THE SAMURAI
AND THE SACRED

OSPREY
PUBLISHING

THE SAMURAI AND THE SACRED

STEPHEN TURNBULL

First published in Great Britain in 2006 by Osprey Publishing, Midland House,
West Way, Botley, Oxford OX2 0PH, United Kingdom.
443 Park Avenue South, New York, NY 10016, USA.
Email: info@ospreypublishing.com

This paperback edition published 2009 by Osprey Publishing Ltd.

A CIP catalogue record for this book is available from the British Library

ISBN: 978 1 84603 215 8

Stephen Turnbull has asserted his right under the Copyright, Designs and Patents Act, 1988, to be
identified as the author of this book.

Page layout by Ken Vail Graphic Design, Cambridge, UK
Index by Alan Thatcher
Typeset in Centaur MT and Malibu
Originated by United Graphic Pte Ltd., Singapore
Printed in China through World Print Ltd.

09 10 11 12   10 9 8 7 6 5 4 3 2 1

For a catalogue of all books published by Osprey please contact:

NORTH AMERICA
Osprey Direct c/o Random House Distribution Center
400 Hahn Road, Westminster, MD 21157, USA
uscustomerservice@ospreypublishing.com

ALL OTHER REGIONS
Osprey Direct, The Book Service Ltd, Distribution Centre, Colchester Road, Frating Green, Colchester,
Essex, CO7 7DW
E-mail: customerservice@ospreypublishing.com

www.ospreypublishing.com

Front cover: Yamaji Masakuni (1546-83) who was killed in battle, shown here fighting an invisible
opponent. The perfect embodiment of the samurai image, he also resembles guardian Nió statues, or an
actor in a Noh play frozen for an expressive moment. The inclusion of a branch of flowering azalea speaks
to the ruthlessness and delicacy of the samurai's life.

Editor's note: All photographs are from the author's collection unless credited otherwise.

CONTENTS

INTRODUCTION

In the year 1592, as the Japanese invasion fleet was about to set sail to attack Korea, there was a slight pause in the proceedings while Matsuura Hōin Shigenobu (1549–1614) performed a brief religious ritual. Dressed in his finest robes and holding aloft a *heihaku* (a symbolic offering made of paper), he climbed up on to the raised deck of his ship and turned to face in the general direction of the distant Iwashimizu shrine, which was dedicated to Hachiman, the *kami* (god) of war. He bowed three times. Guns were fired and his followers gave three war cries. Shigenobu's commander-in-chief, Toyotomi Hideyoshi (1536–98), sent a messenger to enquire after the reason for the noise. Shigenobu reported back that on board his ship they were paying their respects to the Hachiman shrine in acknowledgement of the similar occasion in ancient times when the Empress Jingū had led an invasion of Korea. Toyotomi Hideyoshi was delighted.[1]

This little ceremony, performed at the start of what was to prove one of Japan's cruellest and most disastrous wars, provides a neat illustration of the subtle relationship between the samurai and the sacred. At the heart of the interaction taking place on board Shigenobu's ship is the worship of and reverence for one of the *kami*, the numinous entities that are the focus of worship in the religious system that is known as Shintō. *Kami* is often translated simply as 'god', and the word 'Shintō' means 'the way of the gods'.

Since the 8th century AD Japan has often been referred to in official documents as 'the land of the gods' (*shinkoku*),[2] and any interested visitor to Japan nowadays cannot help being struck by the apparent all-pervasiveness of the sacred in modern Japanese life. Shintō shrines (*jinja*) large and small appear to be everywhere, from household altars to huge architectural complexes. Shrines also exist as tiny memorials on beaches, where anonymous victims of drownings are enshrined, and can even be found within the precincts of the Buddhist temples, which provide another very prominent visual reminder of the enduring religious life of the Japanese people. But sacred objects do not end there. One comes across little stone statues by the roadside, while the courtyards of temples and shrines appear to house fortune-tellers' booths. Wandering monks dressed in full medieval robes turn up in the doorways of restaurants to bless the diners. New cars are ceremoniously purified, and the spires of Christian churches may occasionally be seen protruding from hillsides behind shrines to Confucius.

This situation of apparent harmony has been dubbed 'the Japanese religious supermarket', where, with some notable exceptions, not only have the various religious traditions intermingled throughout history, but Japanese people today also seem happy to participate in rituals from different systems. As the popular saying tells us, the Japanese are 'born Shintō and die Buddhist', with perhaps a wedding in a Christian church somewhere along the journey of life. This accommodative approach to religion has been seen as an example of an assimilative tendency in Japanese culture, whereby 'newly introduced traditions did not uproot the indigenous but were invariably assimilated into a kind of homogeneous tradition which might itself be called Japanese religion'.[3]

Matsuura Shigenobu's spontaneous act of devotion to the *kami* as he was about to set off to war provides an illustration of how religion has permeated

Matsuura Hōin Shigenobu, *daimyō* of Hirado, who prayed for victory before taking part in Hideyoshi's invasion of Korea in 1592. From a painted scroll in the Matsuura Historical Museum, Hirado.

Japanese society throughout history. The world of the samurai and the world of the sacred were not opposing entities. Instead, the two aspects coalesced into one unitary world view where the denizens of the spirit world interacted with men. The *kami* may have been mysterious, but they were also accessible and could be moved to anger or compassion according to whether they were honoured or neglected.

Shigenobu has prudently honoured one very powerful *kami* by his prayers, and will set off on his expedition confident that Hachiman will aid him. Here we see an interesting emphasis being laid upon precedent and tradition. Shigenobu wishes his military expedition to be a success, so he invokes the example of a previous triumph in the same direction by choosing to honour one *kami* in particular. Hachiman is the deified spirit of Emperor Ojin, who lived between AD 201 and 310 according to the traditional reckoning. When his mother, Empress Jingū, carried out her own legendary invasion of Korea she was pregnant with the future emperor and put a stone in her sash to delay his birth.[4] Hachiman, as Japan's primary 'god of war', was therefore a very suitable *kami* to invoke before an invasion. The imperial connection further exemplifies one other very important characteristic of Shintō: its close links with the emperors of Japan, who claimed a direct descent from Amaterasu, the 'Sun-Goddess' – the greatest of all the *kami*.

It is also noticeable that Shigenobu's offering to Hachiman is a very low-key and informal affair. As on so many other occasions throughout history, we see less evidence of a 'religious service' in the Christian sense than an example of an individual turning to the *kami* in times of personal need. Nowadays people visit Shintō shrines at certain times, such as for festivals and personal rites of passage, as well as casually dropping in to pray. Matsuura Shigenobu is praying for victory in battle: a common occurrence in the history of the samurai that often involved a visit to an important shrine where a particular *kami* had been enshrined. When Oda Nobunaga (1534–82) set out on the march that led to his victory at the battle of Okehazama in 1560, he wrote a prayer for victory and deposited it at the Atsuta shrine near present-day Nagoya. Takeda Katsuyori

The Isaniwa shrine in Dōgo Onsen, Matsuyama, dedicated to Hachiman, the important *kami* of war. This shrine was built in 1667.

9

The spire of the Xavier Memorial Chapel, the Catholic church in Hirado, is visible behind the local Buddhist temple.

made a point of visiting the shrine of his father, the late Takeda Shingen, before setting off on the fateful campaign that ended in his defeat at the battle of Nagashino in 1575. In the case cited above, Shigenobu is unable to visit the Iwashimizu shrine, which is located hundreds of miles away near Kyōto, so he bows in its direction.

Finally, the name of Hōin, which is included in Matsuura Shigenobu's title, indicates that in addition to being the leader of an army of samurai he is also a Buddhist priest, thus showing the characteristic blending of and interchange between different Japanese religious traditions. This image of a Buddhist priest apparently performing a ritual from a different religion is a strange concept for a Westerner to understand. No Muslim cleric, for example, would say Mass. But in Shigenobu's day there was little practical distinction between Buddhism and Shintō, and he would also have addressed his patron as *bosatsu* (bodhissatva), a title that gave Hachiman a role in the Buddha's mission to save all beings.[5]

There appears to be no expression of any religious traditions in Shigenobu's ritual other than Shintō and Buddhist elements, but examples of other spiritual perspectives are not hard to find elsewhere in Japanese history. The monk Saichō (767–822), the founder of the Tendai sect of Buddhism, chose Mount Hiei as the location for his temple of Enryakuji: a foundation that was to have an enormous influence on Japanese religion for centuries to come. He chose it

A tiny wayside shrine beside the road in Kyōto. Flowers and an apple have been left as offerings.

partly because it was a holy mountain that was the abode of *kami,* but also because of Taoist beliefs in lucky directions. A few centuries later, Mount Hiei's most notorious denizens, its armies of *sōhei* (warrior monks), would march into battle carrying portable shrines dedicated to the *kami* that was enshrined on the mountain. Both through their dual roles as priests and warriors, and through their use of Shintō emblems, the *sōhei* provided a dramatic illustration of the complex and intertwined nature of the samurai and the sacred.

This book aims to tell the story of this subtle relationship as it developed throughout Japanese history. The samurai is often seen as almost exclusively a fighting man. Here the depths of faith and culture that supported his better-known role will be revealed. It begins with the world of gods and spirits that permeated every element of the samurai's career from birth to death, and includes the influence that this religious milieu exerted upon him as a warrior, an administrator and a patron of the arts. From the battlefield to the tea house and back again, this book explores, for example, how the samurai expressed the ideals of Zen Buddhism and Confucianism in his roles as swordsman and leader. The plays he enjoyed in the theatre, the gardens in which he meditated, the way he performed at archery and even the manner in which he was expected to depart this life ensured that the life of a samurai was acted out with the rich colours of a vibrant sacredness.

THE WAY OF
THE GODS

The worship of the *kami* was practised for centuries before other religions entered the Japanese scene, and even to the most casual visitor to Japan today, 'the way of the gods' appears to have very ancient and deep-rooted foundations. The proliferation of Shintō shrines in Japan, their presence usually indicated by the presence of a *torii* (a gateway in the shape of the Greek letter 'pi'), leads any visitor to think that the religion *kami* represent is a long-established, crucial element of Japanese culture, providing it with a distinctive religious system found nowhere else on earth. Just as in the example of Matsuura Shigenobu, the *kami* are prayed to so that they will provide blessings of a this-world variety, such as success in exams and easy childbirth.[1] On visiting a Shintō shrine people wash their hands and rinse their mouths in a sacred fountain. Coins are thrown into a box as an offering, and the bell is rung to summon the *kami*. Hands are clapped and heads are bowed.

Further observation, particularly of festival rites, suggests that Shintō bears some of the characteristics of primitive animistic belief. The worship of nature, the offering of food to the *kami*, the avoidance of impurity and the observance of rituals to correct a failure in this regard are its stock in trade. Shintō also appears to incorporate the worship of thousands of gods who are not necessarily either immortal or omnipotent. It has a pronounced local flavour, yet possesses powerful features associated otherwise with organized religion, such as a central organization, an ordained priesthood and numerous festivals on its calendar that are observed in similar ways across the nation. *Kannushi* (Shintō priests) wear striking traditional costumes of black *eboshi* hats and white robes, and project a

OPPOSITE

A *torii* gateway under snow at the Shintō shrine on Mount Iimori, Aizu-Wakamatsu.

13

dignity that is universally respected. Most importantly to the casual observer, Shintō gives the overriding impression of being somehow very, very Japanese.[2]

A brief examination of the literature available strengthens the initial impression that Shintō is Japan's 'national religion'. Its mythology seems to be concerned exclusively with the Japanese people and their environment, and the lively Shintō creation myths deal only with the creation of Japan, not any wider world. When sociological surveys are taken virtually all Japanese identify themselves with Shintō, so to some meaningful extent Shintō and being Japanese are synonymous. These casual impressions also appear to be confirmed by the official presentation of Shintō to the curious outsider. For example, a pamphlet published many years ago by the Jinja Honchō (the Association of Shintō Shrines, to which 75 per cent of all shrines belong),[3] sums up the origin of Shintō for English-speaking visitors as follows:

> Shinto is a general term for the activities of the Japanese people to worship all the deities of heaven and earth, and its origin is as old as the history of the Japanese. It was towards the end of the sixth century when the Japanese were conscious of these activities and called them 'Way of the Kami'. It coincides with the time when the 31st Emperor Yomei prayed before an image of the Buddha [for] the first time as an emperor for recovery of his illness. Thus accepting Buddhism, a foreign religion, the Japanese realised [the] existence of a tradition of their own faith.[4]

The famous 'floating *torii*' of the Itsukushima shrine on the island of Miyajima, shown at low tide.

This paragraph is very interesting, because it states that it was only necessary to give a name to this supposedly indigenous belief system when there was a pressing need to distinguish it from the recently imported religion of Buddhism. Also, even though no less a person than the emperor chose to pray before an image of the Buddha, he was not thereby renouncing the existing religious tradition of Shintō. This would have been impossible, because he was its most important living symbol, a status that had come about because of the existence of a complex mythology that linked the imperial line to the *kami*. This is a vitally important topic in Shintō studies which this book will address. For now we may note that as the descendant of *kami*, Emperor Yomei (who is supposed to have reigned between 585 and 587) was in the distinguished, if somewhat bewildering, company of tens of thousands of deified spirits. Their vast range was neatly summed up by the scholar Motoori Norinaga (1730–1801), who provided this classic definition of *kami*:

> first of all, deities of heaven and earth and spirits venerated at shrines, as well as humans, birds and beasts, plants and trees, oceans and mountains that have exceptional powers and ought to be revered. Kami include not only mysterious beings that are noble and good but also malignant spirits that are extraordinary and deserve veneration.[5]

A strangely shaped rock formation could therefore indicate the presence of a *kami*, while thunder was known as 'the *kami* that rumbles'. Yet not all spiritual entities were *kami*. *Tama* (souls) and *oni* (demons), among other things, had a spiritual existence, and out of the vast crowd of spiritual possibilities certain entities were chosen and elevated in rank to a position where they were regarded as having power over other spirits. So the *kami* of a particular mountain was believed to control the animal and spiritual life of its locality. Mount Omiwa in Nara Prefecture, for example, is still venerated as the abode of a *kami*, and, unlike most Shintō shrines, there is no main hall for enshrining the *kami* because the mountain itself is its home. Its status as a 'holy mountain' is therefore broadly understandable to a foreign visitor, even though the practical expression of its veneration is more extreme than, say, Egypt's Mount Sinai:

> It is not very big in scale, but has kept up its pure figure through the vicissitudes of its long history. To this day, people… have never tried to step into the mountain, because it is a holy site, though Mt. Miwa is not enclosed by fence or palisades. Therefore, the trees are never cut down and the whole mountain is covered by virgin woods.[6]

Similar respect for other 'holy sites' is often remarked upon by foreign visitors and extends to small wayside shrines where there is a noticeable absence of graffiti and vandalism.

A Shintō shrine has somehow been fitted into this urban landscape next to an office block.

In a later stage of historical development some powerful *kami* were given names and adopted as tutelary deities by important families. In this way Hachiman, with his clear military connections, became the *kami* to be associated in particular with the powerful Minamoto family, whose son Yoritomo was to become Japan's first hereditary *sei-i-taishōgun* (military dictator or 'Shogun') in 1192. But the Minamoto were not alone in their adoption of Hachiman. Matsuura Shigenobu clearly had a personal affinity towards him, while Okochi Hidemoto, another participant in Hideyoshi's Korean invasion, shared Hachiman as his family's personal *kami*. In a break from the fighting to capture the Korean town of Namweon in 1597, Okochi Hidemoto took a moment to honour Hachiman:

> Graciously calling to mind that this day was the fifteenth day of the eighth lunar month, the day dedicated to his tutelary *kami* Hachiman Daibosatsu, he put down his bloodstained blade and, pressing his crimson stained palms, bowed in veneration towards far-off Japan.[7]

THE IMPERIAL CONNECTION

Out of all the tutelary *kami* adopted and revered by various families and their descendants, no connection is more important than the link made between Amaterasu, Japan's 'Sun-Goddess', and the ruling imperial line. But the successive emperors of Japan – the members of the world's longest surviving ruling house – do not claim merely to have adopted Amaterasu as their tutelary *kami*. Instead they have proudly proclaimed over the centuries an actual lineal descent from her. This is a divine ancestry that justifies the temporal power that they have enjoyed for so long, and has certainly helped preserve the dynasty, even if some of its members were deposed, banished and in one case, drowned.[8]

The earliest written accounts that make this claim date from the 8th century, by which time the imperial house was well established and Japan had embraced Buddhism and its associated Chinese culture. The sources include two important semi-historical works called the *Kojiki* (712) and the *Nihon shoki* (720), which were compiled under the guidance and direction of the imperial court. At first sight these 'Books of Genesis', which begin with the creation of the universe and move inexorably to the establishment of the ruling house, are works of colourful mythology. But they were also political propaganda, whereby several powerful myths, hitherto unrelated but now combined into a strong narrative, were used to justify the supremacy of one family – the 'Yamato Court' – over all others.

Dancers at the Fushimi Inari shrine near Kyōto.

This is not to say that these stories were deliberately invented by the imperial scribes. It is more likely that the tales already existed as animistic legends told by farmers and fishermen who venerated their own local *kami*.[9]

The *Kojiki* version may be summarized briefly as follows. After a succession of generations of creator *kami*, the husband and wife Izanagi and Izanami give birth to the main islands of Japan. Izanami then brings forth the *kami* of fire and is burned to death. Izanagi goes in search of her in the land of the dead. Upon his return, he purifies himself in the ocean, an action that results in the creation of three important *kami*, each born from a different part of his body: Amaterasu, the Sun-Goddess, Tsukuyomi and Susa-no-o, to whom are allotted the three parts of the universe. Susa-no-o exhibits violent behaviour, which alarms his sister Amaterasu so much that she takes refuge in a cave. The world is therefore plunged into darkness and her fellow *kami* try desperately to entice her out. As a trick, Amaterasu is told that a rival *kami* even more powerful than she has arrived. Her interest aroused, she peeps cautiously out of the cave. The first things she sees are a precious jewel hanging from a tree and, next to it, the face of her new rival. This makes her start, and she is grabbed before she has time to realize that what she is actually looking at is her own reflection in a bronze mirror. Light is therefore restored to the world.

Susa-no-o takes a more positive role when he destroys a monstrous serpent that is terrorizing the people. As he reaches its tail, his blade meets with unexpected resistance, and Susa-no-o discovers a sword hidden therein. As it is a very fine sword he presents it to his sister, Amaterasu.[10] Amaterasu in turn gives the sword to her grandson, Ninigi, who descends from heaven to rule the

A typical small Shintō shrine.

A young visitor to a
Shintō shrine drinks
from the sacred fountain,
where one also rinses
one's hands.

earth. Ninigi eventually passes it on to his grandson, Jimmu, identified as the
first *tennō* (emperor) of Japan, to whom are given the traditional dates of
660–585 BC. Jimmu Tennō keeps this sword as one of the three 'crown jewels'
of the Japanese emperors. The mirror and the jewel that had restored light to
the world become the other items in the imperial regalia.

By the time of these writings, the imperial line had faced many challenges to
its supremacy. The rival clans who opposed the Yamato Court had their own
creation myths and their own tutelary *kami*, as may be deduced from reading
between the lines of the *Kojiki* account.[11] A particular current of rivalry is
suggested in the narratives concerned with the *kami* Susa-no-o. He is presented
negatively as an unruly rebel and positively as a dragon-slaying hero, but he
eventually submits to the authority of Amaterasu. Susa-no-o is associated with
the important Izumo area of Japan (modern Shimane Prefecture), where he is
honoured as the region's cultural hero who brought knowledge of metal-working.
As the myth finishes with the agreement of Susa-no-o's descendant to yield the
territory of Izumo to the Yamato line and build a grand shrine there, we may see
within the story a re-telling of the political subordination of the sun line's
greatest domestic rival.[12]

To counter opponents like the Izumo chieftains, the Yamato line harnessed
both the sacred and the samurai. The term 'samurai' was coming into use to
describe the elite mounted warriors used by the emperors to enforce their rule.
With the samurai as their army, their bodyguards and their policemen, the
emperors ruled through a political structure based on successful Chinese
models of governance. In this context it is interesting to note that one
particular Chinese political tradition was decisively rejected by the Yamato
emperors. Early in Chinese history, the idea had developed that the person who

ascended the throne possessed the 'mandate of heaven'. This implied that if heaven withdrew its mandate then the ruling house could be legitimately overthrown and be replaced, as was the case with successive Chinese dynasties. In marked contrast the Japanese creation myths recognized the emperor as the highest Shintō priest in the land who was descended from the greatest *kami* of all. This gave the Yamato rulers a permanent heavenly mandate.

The grafting of a system of imperial self-justification on to a stock of well-established localized folk-beliefs about *kami* — beliefs that were so much taken for granted that there was no need to give them a name — was to have fateful results many centuries later. In 1868, after the last Tokugawa Shogun had been overthrown in favour of a restored imperial power, there was an enforced separation of Shintō and Buddhism and the creation of purely Shintō shrines with no Buddhist elements within them. The founding fathers of modern Japan therefore made Shintō into a state cult of imperial veneration. They also made it serve nationalistic ends and used it to justify military aggression overseas. Motoori Norinaga, whose definition of *kami* was cited above, was a scholar whose work was to influence the restoration movement. He was clearly under no personal illusions when he wrote the following:

The inner courtyard of the Isonokami shrine near Tenri, showing casks of *sake* left as offerings.

Our country's Imperial Line, which casts its light over this world, represents the descendants of the Sky-Shining Goddess. And in accordance with that Goddess's mandate of reigning 'for ever and ever, coeval with Heaven and earth', the Imperial

Line is destined to rule the nation for ever until the end of time and as long as the universe exists. That is the very basis of our Way. That our history has not deviated from the instructions of the divine mandate bears testimony to the infallibility of our ancient tradition. It can also be seen why foreign countries cannot match ours…[13]

This is a classic exposition of Shintō in its bombastic nationalist guise, and passages such as these, when contrasted with the rustic simplicity of a village shrine, can only serve to increase the confusion over what Shintō actually is. Is it 'a relic of ancient nature worship' or 'an outdated invented tradition'?[14] The most extreme position on this was taken by Kuroda Toshio, who regarded both the indigenous nature of Shintō and its supposed uniqueness as being largely a modern construction dating from the time of Japan's re-emergence into the wider world. Something that had never really existed before 1868 was invented and given the label of 'Shintō' to justify the new powers exercised by the emperor. Belief in a continuous Shintō tradition was therefore no more than belief in a ghostly image.[15]

Kuroda did not deny that the worship of *kami* had gone on for centuries. Rather, he saw them as occupying a central role in pre-modern Japanese religious life as a way of localizing and integrating Buddhist worship into the Japanese milieu. All of what is commonly regarded as Shintō was *kami* worship carried out side by side with the worship of Buddha, not as a compromise but as a well-integrated whole. The historical position has been expressed succinctly as follows:

A Shintō priest carrying a *gohei* (the ceremonial 'wand' used to give blessings).

> The fact of the matter is that Buddhist monks in pre-modern Japan were also Shintoists, which is to say no more — but no less — than that they were enmeshed from birth in a cultural fabric that was shot through with a melange of indigenous and imported myths, symbols, rituals and moods that taken together we call Shinto. Throughout most of Japanese history, foreign (Buddhist, but also Taoist and Confucian) and indigenous elements were amalgamated in a single cohesive whole. Indeed, Buddhism and Shinto were amalgamated institutionally, ritually, and doctrinally to such a degree that to treat them as distinct, independent traditions is to misrepresent the structure of pre-modern Japanese societies.[16]

In this way not only did Buddhism influence Shintō — Shintō also caused the transformation of Buddhism within Japanese culture. There may have been differences between the sorts of rituals that Shintō and Buddhism carried out, but they were functional differences rather than ones that could be labelled 'sectarian'.[17]

A golden Shintō *gohei* was used as a battle standard by Shibata Katsuie. In this print his standard-bearer Menju Ietora fights bravely to rescue it from the enemy.

Modern research, unfettered by the nationalism of the mid-20th century, tends to see Shintō as a complex religious phenomenon, and questions the understanding that the Japanese people have of themselves in relation to Shintō. Many Japanese people participate in a large number of Shintō festivals and rituals, such as shrine-visiting at New Year, a time when a casual visitor to the Inner Shrine at Ise receives the impression that half the Japanese population has come along too. No Japanese people, however, would profess affiliation to 'the Shintō religion'. *Kami* worship is more like an undercurrent to the business of being Japanese, expressing a concept of worship that is very different from conventional Western ideas of religious behaviour and belief. Modern research leads to many conclusions about Shintō's complex origins that go far beyond the imperial creation myths.[18]

THE ORIGINS OF THE KAMI

If Shintō is itself difficult to define, the same applies to the deities that are its focus. Among the notable differences between Japanese and Western thinking about religion is a willingness to accept comparatively imprecise definitions of the nature of its gods. *Kami* never seem to be precisely identified, and it is sometimes difficult to avoid a circular reasoning that defines Shintō as the worship of *kami* and then defines *kami* as that which is worshipped in Shintō, although this vagueness somehow manages to express something of the true *kami* nature.[19]

Any modern searches for the origin of the *kami* must begin with certain archaeological artefacts that suggest a use for religious purposes. Without written evidence, however, we can only speculate as to how such a religion was practised, and whether any entities resembling *kami* provided its focus. As time went by two distinctive pottery-producing cultures emerged. The first was the Neolithic Jōmon culture (*c.* 10,000–300 BC). It was initially a hunter/gatherer culture, followed by primitive agriculture, and excavations of Jōmon sites have yielded some very striking clay figurines called *dogū*. Nearly all depict women with exaggerated breasts and distended abdomens suggestive of pregnancy. Some have been accorded special care, having been placed on a platform,[20] and it has been suggested that the *dogū* represent female deities who managed procreation.[21]

The Yayoi culture (*c.* 300 BC–AD 300) that succeeded the Jōmon era was based around a developed agricultural system that concentrated on the cultivation of rice. Bronze and iron tools were used in rice growing, and divination was practised by shamans who interpreted the cracks that resulted from heating deer bones.[22] The Yayoi people also used tools that were probably imported from

The developed form of Shintō shrine-building is illustrated here by the Oagata shrine near Komaki.

mainland China and Korea. These included iron shovels and ploughs, but bronze mirrors and bell-like ritual objects were also an important part of their lives.[23]

We know far more about the Yayoi Period because of accounts written by Chinese visitors to Japan. One, the *Wei Zhi* (History of the Kingdom of Wei) of *c.* 297 AD, describes a female ruler of Japan called Pimiko who practised shamanism.[24] Bell-shaped bronzes called *dōtaku* are also found in Yayoi sites and appear to have been used for ceremonial and religious purposes,[25] but the most striking link from the Yayoi Period to what we now call Shintō lies in the design of the earliest Shintō shrines, which emerged a few centuries later and show a debt to Yayoi culture. The erection of buildings to make a *jinja* (shrine) where 'the *kami* is venerated at a place of his own selection, rather than that of man' is a later development in Japanese religious history.[26] Because the most ancient form of sacred space had been a tree, a stone or some other natural phenomenon, many shrines incorporated their natural surroundings into their design, as they still do today, sometimes with the sole addition of a small *hokora* (a small stone shrine with a sloping roof).

Archaeologists believe that the distinctive style of the shrines at Ise is typical of rice storehouse construction during the Yayoi Period. An image of one storehouse appears on a cast bronze bell discovered on the island of Shikoku.[27] Ise, the location of the enshrinement of Amaterasu, consists of two shrines: one to Amaterasu and the other to Toyouke, the *kami* of food. According to a long tradition the two shrines were alternately rebuilt after a period of 20 years in an exact replica of the building that came before – a simple wooden structure consisting of a high pitched roof and a raised floor.

A *kamidana*, the household 'god shelf' whereby Shintō has a place in the family home.

A very dramatic change in the religious landscape in Japan came in about AD 300 with the building of the first *kofun* (large burial tumuli). Those constructed to house the remains of emperors are enormous, often 200m (656ft) long. Some are shaped like a keyhole, and many form artificial islands within a lake. The time of their construction, between 300 and 646, is known as the Kofun Period, and the grave goods and evidence of funerary practices show a considerable religious aspect to the times.[28] Queen Pimiko's burial rites are described in the same Chinese chronicle noted above, which tells us how 'a great mound was raised over her more than a hundred paces in diameter and over a hundred of her male and female attendants followed her in death'. The few *kofun* that have been excavated reveal that armour, harnesses, weapons, bronze mirrors and jewels were buried with the deceased. On top of the tombs or inside them were placed *haniwa*, primitive but lifelike clay models of soldiers, servants and animals, which may have their origins as substitutes for the human sacrifice described in the account of Queen Pimiko's death. Together with the real weapons buried in the tombs, the *haniwa* show that these early aristocrats eventually became mounted warriors – the ancestors of the samurai. The articles found inside the tombs indicate both a sophisticated production system in Japan and close trading links with continental Asia.[29]

Even though the number of artefacts associated with *kofun* burials is large, it is difficult on this basis alone to identify the specific *kami* that are connected with the sites other than the august person who is buried there. By this time, however, the ranking of the *kami* had begun, and the routes by which certain *kami* had entered the realm of humans were beginning to be identified. Some

There is a great similarity in style between the design of the earliest Shintō shrines and that of the rice storehouses constructed during the Yayoi Period. Here two storehouses have been reconstructed at the important archaeological site of Yoshinogari, which may be the seat of the legendary Queen Pimiko.

25

The main building of the Kasuga shrine at Nara, founded in 709 by Fujiwara Fuhito to enshrine the tutelary *kami* of the Fujiwara family. It has close associations with the Buddhist Kōfukuji nearby.

came from the mountains, others from the sea. Particular reverence also grew for the *yorishiro*, the symbolic object in which the *kami* settled.[30] A useful metaphor, although one to be applied with care, sees the *yorishiro* as a 'landing site', with the ritual purification of the sacred area as an act of 'trapping the power of the divinity within the sacred space'.[31]

In some mysterious way the *kami* both inhabit their shrines and act at a distance from the place they reside.[32] So, for example, it is not the Sun-Goddess herself who dwells in the Ise shrine. Her true place is in heaven, but she is present in some way on earth, as is proved by her answering the prayers that are made to her at the shrine. The *goshintai* (the 'body of the god' – the object in the shrine that provides the precise location of the *kami*) may be clearly identified, such as the sacred mountain of Omiwa, but more often it is an object that remains hidden inside the shrine, wrapped in a succession of unopened caskets and cloths, sometimes with its actual identity unknown even to the priests who are its guardians. Of known objects, many are mirrors, while other *goshintai* include swords, stones and in one case an iron ball. They are often carried in the ceremonial palanquins called *mikoshi*, the portable shrines paraded during a shrine's annual *matsuri* (festival) in a journey that may include a visit to the place where the object was originally found. Elaborate ritual precautions are taken to hide a *goshintai* from human eyes when it is being transferred from a shrine building, even though it may be securely wrapped. As recently as 1967 cars in Nara still had to put out their lights within the radius of half a mile from a certain shrine when transference was taking place.[33]

Shintō *kannushi* (priests) of the Omiwa shrine, dressed in full robes for the shrine's spring *matsuri* (festival).

By the end of the Kofun Period Shintō was well on its way to becoming an institutionalized religion that supported the imperial hegemony without losing its agricultural and fertility roots. Perhaps the most significant ritual to demonstrate the continuing link was the *Daijōsai*, a ceremony held at the time of a new emperor's accession to the throne, during which the new monarch shared with the *kami* a meal prepared from rice grown in consecrated fields. By the end of the 6th century, however, the *kami* no longer had it all their own way. Foreign beliefs had arrived in the land of the gods.

27

BUDDHA AND THE BUSHI

The religion of Buddhism was founded in India by Sākyamuni, an Indian prince who pondered on the nature of human suffering, which to him seemed to be everywhere. With his conclusion – that the reason for suffering was human desire, and that desire was itself illusory because, as nothing is permanent, nothing can ever be possessed – he achieved enlightenment and became Buddha ('The Enlightened One').

In the 3rd century BC, King Aśoka, the third monarch of the Indian Mauryan dynasty, converted to Buddhism and the teaching spread. Over the next two centuries a movement called Mahāyāna Buddhism developed, which incorporated local deities into its pantheon much as the *kami* were to be brought into Japanese Buddhism. When these were combined with a belief in the different manifestations of Buddha, it resulted in a growing list of names through which Buddha was worshipped and invoked. In Japan these would include Shaka, the historical Buddha; Amida, the dispenser of infinite love; Miroku, the Buddha of the Future; Yakushi Nyorai, the healing Buddha, and so on, as well as Kannon, the Goddess of Mercy, and Fudō, the 'immoveable one': two deities borrowed from outside Buddhism.

The faith entered China during the 1st century AD. The scriptures were translated into Chinese, and as China's neighbours were heavily influenced by Chinese culture Buddhism spread widely, reaching Korea around the 4th and 5th centuries, and Japan around the middle of the 6th century.

The introduction of Buddhism into Japan provided a religious system that many regarded as a rival and an act of effrontery to the *kami*. However, the

OPPOSITE

The association between Chinese culture and the Japanese imperial family of the Nara Period is beautifully illustrated here at the Zenkōji in Nagano. In this picture we see two *komainu* (Chinese dogs) in front of a curtain bearing the imperial chrysanthemum.

A statue of Kannon, the Goddess of Mercy, in the courtyard of the Eiheiji on the island of Ikitsuki.

emperors, who were Shintō's guardians and in many ways its main beneficiaries, eventually came to view Buddhism in a very positive light as an integral part of the Chinese culture that was being absorbed into Japan with beneficial results. Buddhism offered a metaphysical world view based on sophisticated teachings that went far beyond the animistic myths of early Japan. It also provided a form of magic that ensured the welfare of the emperor and of the state.

The 'official date' for the introduction of Buddhism into Japan is given in the *Nihon shoki* as 552, which is probably accurate, as the new religion seems to have appeared during the reign of Emperor Kinmei (ruled 539–571). Certain clans, notably the Soga family, who built the first full-scale Buddhist temple in Japan, were more enthusiastic about embracing Buddhism than was the imperial court, so the introduction of Buddhism split the ruling class of Japan. Buddhism became a matter of great controversy, as did the Korean king's gift of a statue of Buddha, which ended up being unceremoniously dumped into a canal. It was soon retrieved, and is now housed within the great Zenkōji temple in Nagano. The war for Buddhism ended in a victory in 587 for Soga Umako, but in spite of his decisive role in establishing Buddhism in Japan another name is far more closely associated with the spread of Buddhism: Prince Shōtoku (572–621). Having ruled as regent from 593, Shōtoku, whose life has probably been embellished by legend, declared Buddhism to be the state religion in Japan. Of all the many Buddhist foundations associated with Shōtoku's religious and political reforms, none is more celebrated than the beautiful temple of Hōryūji near Nara, the world's oldest wooden building.[1]

By the end of the first hundred years of Buddhism's existence in Japan, its influence had spread widely in both geographical and social terms. 'State Buddhism', in the sense of imperial patronage, began under Emperor Jomei (ruled 629–641) with his foundation of the first national temple in 639. Recent excavation of the site has revealed a very large religious complex.[2] This building represented the physical manifestation of a number of state-sponsored initiatives designed to actively promote Buddhism in Japan, such as the copying of sutras, the support for rituals and the foundation of other temples and statues.

In 646 the government announced the Taika reforms, an ambitious set of edicts that theoretically made all of Japan subject to the emperor. One of the

The Zenkōji at Nagano, seen here under snow, houses the original statue of Buddha sent from Korea.

first tasks of the reformers was to establish Japan's first permanent capital city. This was achieved, after a couple of false starts, at Nara in 710. The city was laid out on a grid plan imitating that of the capital of the Tang Dynasty of China, from which Japan's rulers drew their inspiration for making their ordered state into a reflection of the Buddhist world order. The statesman Fujiwara Fuhito (659–720) encouraged the move to Nara by founding the Buddhist temple of Kōfukuji and the Shintō Kasuga shrine as the spiritual guardians of the new capital.[3] Fuhito also protected his family's position by methodically marrying off his daughters to Japanese emperors, and it was his grandson Emperor Shōmu, who reigned from 724 to 749, who was to provide Nara with its largest and most glorious monument: the Buddhist temple of Tōdaiji, built to house a colossal image of Buddha. It was 16m (52ft) high and the largest cast product of the ancient world.[4]

In the buildings of Tōdaiji and Kōfukuji the sacred function was exercised on a grand scale that befitted the capital of Japan. In 752 Tōdaiji, which rivalled the greatest Chinese monuments, was inaugurated in the most splendid ceremony ever witnessed in Japan, and the shrines of the *kami* now had a magnificent rival. Within the Daibutsuden, the main hall of Tōdaiji, the central figure of Vairocana Buddha surrounded by his manifestations seemed to the emperor to be a divine guarantor of the similarly central position he occupied in the Japanese hegemony. By such arguments Buddhism could be used to support the imperial supremacy, but Shintō, through its myths of descent from Amaterasu, provided the ultimate guarantee of its permanence. What is less well known is that

Emperor Shōmu, who reigned from 724 to 749, was to provide Nara with its largest, most glorious monument: the Buddhist temple of Tōdaiji. This is its Daibutsuden, built to house a colossal image of Buddha. The present reconstruction dates from 1709, and is only 40 per cent of the size of the original.

Emperor Shōmu was also ordained as a Buddhist monk. The blending between Buddhism and Shintō could hardly have been more dramatically personified.

By the end of the Nara Period (646–793), which was concluded with the moving of the capital to Heian-kyō (modern Kyōto), their joint patronage meant that Buddhism and Shintō were beginning to form a syncretic system, and the *kami* acquired a new status and new roles. With the compilation of the *Kojiki* and the *Nihon shoki*, the *kami*'s existence as the founders of the imperial house was set in stone, while at the same time their relation to Buddhism was clarified. As sentient beings one stage higher than humans, the *kami* needed the Buddha's salvation, yet they were also seen as the guardians of Buddhist law. Some *kami* were referred to as *bosatsu* (bodhisattvas). When the Tōdaiji was completed, Empress Kōken, Emperor Shōmu's daughter, visited the temple to issue an imperial decree thanking Hachiman for his assistance with the project.[5]

Just as the powerful families who had once challenged the Yamato court had become integrated into its military institutions as *bushi* (warriors – an alternative expression to samurai), so also did they integrate into the political and religious life of the Japanese court. Many of them were fervent supporters of Buddhism, and just like their divine leader in Nara they sponsored the development of

Buddhism in their localities. These initiatives could include lectures from visiting monks and the development of Buddhist activities for the lower orders of society. This aspect of Buddhism, which is often overlooked beside the powerful image of court-based ritual and architecture, is preserved through collections of tales such as the *Nihon Ryōiki*, the earliest anthology of Buddhist stories in Japan. It was compiled by Kyōkai, a priest of the Nara temple of Yakushiji. One story concerns two poor fishermen, lost at sea, who are saved from death by chanting, '*Namu Shakamuni-butsu*' ('Hail to the Buddha Shakamuni'). In another story a miner is similarly saved from death underground through his Buddhist faith. There are also accounts of local cooperation in building a Buddhist temple for a village. Other tales, however, go further than merely affirming the efficacy of faith in Buddha and amount to a slightly veiled attack on the powers and reputation of the *kami*, who are presented as deluded sentient beings. One story tells of a Buddhist priest who is staying at the Shintō Taga shrine in Omi province. The *kami* of the shrine appears to him as a monkey, and explains that he has been made to take this form because of his evil karma. He begs the priest to release him from his present suffering by reciting the Lotus Sutra, the scripture regarded as the true teaching of Buddha.[6]

By the middle of the Heian Period (794–1185), it was clear that such attempts to deprive the *kami* of their dignity were neither effective nor necessary, and the intellectual current of the time moved rapidly towards a philosophy of Shintō/Buddhist syncretism. The result was the *honji suijaku* ('original prototype – local manifestation') theory, which stated that the eternal Buddha, wishing to save all deluded sentient beings, had manifested himself as the *kami*. So, for example, the *kami* of the important Kumano Shingū shrine was identified with Yakushi Nyorai, the Buddha of healing,[7] while the Kasuga shrine in Nara was an earthly depiction of the heavenly paradise of the Buddhist counterparts of the Shintō *kami* enshrined there.[8]

SACRED SPACE

As Buddhism came to Japan by way of China, it is not surprising to find that the model adopted for the general layout of the temples where the new faith was practised was based on Chinese antecedents. The architecture of Chinese Buddhist temples was derived in turn from that of the Chinese palace. By and large, the overall pattern of a Buddhist temple compound that it gave rise to has lasted to this day. There are numerous variations, but certain features have stubbornly persisted over the centuries.

Most Buddhist temples are entered through a formal gateway in the place occupied by a Shintō *torii*. Because this gate symbolically marks the entrance to the precincts it may not even have closing doors or walls on either side. It may also contain a pair of huge statues called *Niō*. These half-naked giants, who stand guard over the temple entrance, are derived from Hindu deities who were incorporated into Buddhist cosmology. One *Niō* has its mouth open, while the other's mouth is closed.

The buildings arranged within the courtyard are solidly framed wooden structures standing on masonry terraces and crowned with graceful tiled roofs. They are built round a framework of massive vertical timbers, with large cross pieces and very intricate bracketing to support upper storeys and roofs. Each vertical support usually rests on one very large stone. The main hall within the courtyard is called the *hondō* (or sometimes the *kondō*). The *hondō* invariably has overhanging eaves protecting an outside walkway that stretches round the building and is reached by a flight of stairs. Some form of door at the front leads to the interior of the *hondō*. This may be a sliding or hinged wooden door or a set of doors, with additional sliding *shōji* doors just inside. *Shōji* are instantly recognizable as light-framed doors with translucent paper covering them. Alternatively, the doors may be hinged at the top, and are lifted up and propped open. The main image in the temple occupies a central place within the *hondō*, while around it is the space for the priests or monks to perform services, together with some provision for lay worshippers to gather. The floor is usually of wooden planking, augmented by *tatami* (straw mats).

Outside in the courtyard there may be some lanterns. A pagoda is often found in the temples of the older sects, but is unusual in Zen or Jōdo Shinshū temples. Pagodas came to Japan with Buddhism itself. Originally towers for housing the remains of the Buddha as relics, they developed for other purposes such as markers for holy places. A very common feature is a free-standing bell tower, with a huge bronze bell that is rung using an external wooden clapper. Temples that also function as monasteries are likely to include a lecture hall, together with other similar buildings concerned with the education and ordination of monks. One may find a sutra (Buddhist scripture) repository, various dormitories, living quarters and a refectory. These buildings usually stand alone, but may be connected to each other using roofed wooden corridors. Further features may include a garden and a Shintō shrine associated with the temple's foundation.[9]

A typical free-standing wooden bell tower, with a bronze bell rung by an external clapper swung on ropes.

MONKS AND MOUNTAINS

In 794 Japan's capital was moved from Nara to Kyōto via the short-term Nagaoka. Kyōto's original name of Heian-kyō was to give its name to the Heian Period in Japanese history. The motive behind the move is usually reckoned to be a desire by the imperial court to free itself from the stranglehold of the great Nara monasteries, but it also followed a change in the genealogical direction of the imperial line.

Before the new site was selected, careful investigations had been undertaken to ensure that the location was suitable according to the Taoist principles of *feng shui* (see pp. 54–55 for more on Taoism). *Feng shui* included the belief that evil could attack a city from a north-easterly direction, where the 'demon gate' is found. To the north-east of Kyōto lies a mountain called Hieizan (Mount Hiei), where there had long been a shrine to a *kami* known as Sannō, 'the king of the mountain'. This was most encouraging, but on top of Mount Hiei there was also a new Buddhist temple called Enryakuji, which had been founded only six years earlier. It owed its existence to the monk Saichō, known to posterity by the name of Dengyō Daishi ('The Great Master Who Transmitted the Teachings').

Saichō had entered the religious life at the tender age of 11. He received full ordination at the age of 18 at Tōdaiji, and shortly afterwards left Nara for the wild Mount Hiei, where he built a simple hermitage: the holy mountain's first religious building after the shrine of Sannō. In 797 Saichō was appointed to a position as court priest, which brought him to the notice of Emperor Kammu (781–806). Sent as a government-sponsored student to Tang China in 804, he returned full of enthusiasm for esoteric Buddhism (*mikkyō*), a passion that was to be shared by his emperor. The result was the founding of the Tendai sect of Buddhism, with its headquarters on Mount Hiei in Saichō's new temple of Enryakuji.

In 806 Saichō successfully petitioned the court for a change in the ordination system. For many years the number of ordinands had been strictly limited to ten. Not only was the number increased to accommodate the Tendai movement, but for the first time the ordinands were assigned to specific 'schools' – a move that effectively signified an

The pagoda of the Toyokawa Inari shrine, which is also a Buddhist temple.

The Heian shrine shown here was built to commemorate the 1,100th anniversary of the founding of Kyōto, and is based on the appearance of the original imperial palace in Heian.

official recognition of sectarianism in Japanese Buddhism.[10] The Tendai sect was intended to operate outside the influence of the Office of Monastic Affairs, which was dominated by Nara. Enryakuji soon became involved in the performance of numerous sacred rituals connected with the imperial court, and it soon achieved recognition as 'the temple for the pacification and protection of the state'.[11] Enryakuji therefore became one of Japan's most privileged foundations, and Saichō and his disciples received the aristocratic support of the Kyōto nobility, who showered wealth upon the temple. By the 11th century the monastery complex on Mount Hiei consisted of about 3,000 buildings. Much property was owned elsewhere in Japan, making Enryakuji a very wealthy place indeed. It was also pre-eminent in the education it provided, and there is hardly a name in the annals of eminent Japanese Buddhist teachers and preachers up to the 15th century who did not at some time in his life study on Mount Hiei. The Tendai sect was absolutely central to Heian Buddhism, and was to be the parent of all the new sects of Buddhism that emerged during the Kamakura Period. Even Nichiren, who reacted so violently against the teachings of Tendai, had at least been through its maw.[12]

In 835 the ordination quota was changed yet again to accommodate the second of the two great sects that emerged at the beginning of the 9th century: Shingon. Shingon was founded by Kūkai (774–835), who is known to history

as the beloved Kōbō Daishi ('The Great Master Who Promulgates the Law'). Born in 774, he accompanied Saichō on his visit to China in 804. He returned in 806 similarly imbued with an enthusiasm for esoteric Buddhism, although his approach was sufficiently different from Saichō's that he was to found a different sect of Buddhism.[13] Like Saichō, Kūkai also retired to the mountains for ascetic practices, but his wilderness was to be found on the island of Shikoku. He then spread esoteric Buddhism throughout Japan, introducing faith in Mahāvairocana (Dainichi). Emperor Saga took an interest in Kūkai's work, and 812 was to find Kūkai performing ceremonies 'for the protection of the country'. In 814 he conducted the first rituals of initiation into one of the great mysteries of the Shingon sect: the concept of the Diamond and Womb mandalas. Kūkai maintained that his mysterious doctrine could not be transmitted without the use of elaborate diagrams and images, and the Shingon mandalas represent an important artistic presentation of Buddhism.[14] The *Kongōkai* (Diamond Mandala) and the *Taizōkai* (Womb Mandala) are representations of the cosmos under the two aspects of potential energy and dynamic manifestation. They existed at one level as holy pictures, but were also tools for interpreting the mystic significance of a spiritual environment. The holy mountain pilgrimage route from Yoshino to Kumano therefore involved a journey that passed through an earthly expression of the two mandalas.

The temple of Enryakuji on Mount Hiei, founded by the monk Saichō, was a key player in the history of Buddhism in Japan. We are looking down on to the Kompon Chūdō (the fundamental central hall) which is the heart of Enryakuji. The original Kompon Chūdō was built by Saichō to house an image of Yakushi Nyorai (the Healing Buddha). The present reconstruction dates from 1642.

In 823 Emperor Saga's patronage led him to present Kūkai with Tōji, one of only two Buddhist temples allowed within the Heian city precincts. In terms of physical influence, therefore, the new Heian government seemed to have succeeded in prising the control of Buddhism out of Nara's clutches. As the new Buddhist sects were esoteric in their approach, stressing the active quest for enlightenment through strenuous austerities and secret rituals, Buddhism's influence on court affairs in Kyōto proved to be as strong as in the days of Nara. Their monks would undertake arduous mountain pilgrimages and perform long, mysterious rituals in their temples for the welfare of the emperor. Mount Hiei was to become famous for its 'marathon monks' who walked the *kaihyōgō*, a prescribed 30km (19 mile) route around the sacred mountain, offering prayers along the way. The most arduous form this devotion takes is the 'thousand day *kaihyōgō*', whereby the exercise is performed for a period of a thousand days within a space of seven years. Only 40 monks have ever completed it since the year 1571.[15]

In architectural terms, the independence from Nara led to the diminution of Chinese styles in the design of the Heian temples and the emergence of a national style. Two other factors led to the temples looking very different from

The *kondō* of the Shingon temple of Tōji in Kyōto, founded by Kōbō Daishi. This building within the extensive grounds dates from 1606 and is shown here during the popular flea market held on the 21st day of each month.

their predecessors in Nara. The first was the association with mountains. The courtyard model of the Buddhist temple seen at Nara had to be modified because of the mountainous terrain, so halls were built on different levels and joined by mountain paths. Enryakuji, for example, was spread out along a vast area of the summit of Hieizan on its peaks and in its wooded valleys.[16] Another difference was to be found in their interior layout. The *mikkyō* sects stressed gradual initiation into secret rites, so the *hondō* of *mikkyō* temples acquired a central barrier that divided the interior into an outer part for the uninitiated and an inner sanctum. At the same time the esoteric demands of the Shingon sect in particular led to the need for a greatly enlarged priestly space where the important rituals could be performed in utmost secrecy. In some cases this led to the creation of new types of temple buildings, such as the *gomadō*, where offerings using fire could be performed in reasonable safety. Nevertheless, anyone such as the author who has personally witnessed the fierce flames of a Shingon *goma* ritual emerges astounded that a building made of wood could ever withstand such treatment.

The Tendai and Shingon temples also took very seriously their role of serving the populace in addition to the needs of the aristocracy. To be available to the laity in order to instruct and enlighten them caused further problems of space that the old Nara models could not accommodate. Pictorial evidence suggests that, like vassals in an imperial audience, any congregation in a Nara temple had to make do with the open air of the courtyard, with perhaps some form of temporary shelter if the weather was inclement. To cope with the conflicting demands of secrecy and education, three improvements in the plan of the *hondō* were attempted during the Heian Period. The first solution was to add an aisle across the front covered by an extension of the main roof. This is the model found in the most important Tendai building of all: the Kompon Chūdō (Central Main Hall) of Enryakuji, founded in 788. The second was the provision of a building just in front of the *hondō*, either free-standing or joined to it by a gallery. This was already common in Shintō shrines, where it was known as a *raidō* or a *haiden*. The final type was to construct a *raidō* as the fore-hall in contact with the main building of the *hondō*, or more simply as an integral part of it under one roof. This model gave the Heian monks the best of both worlds. The laity could be accommodated with ease, while sliding partitions could allow them to be as easily excluded from anything improper for their eyes.[17]

The esoteric nature of Shingon also contributed to the interweaving of Buddhism and Shintō, as the holy environments of the Diamond and Womb mandalas were extended to include the layout and architecture of Shintō shrines such as the 'paradise world' of Kasuga.[18] Through these considerations esoteric Buddhism influenced Shintō. This happened particularly through a development known as Ryōbu Shintō (Dual Shintō). This was a form of Shintō/Buddhist syncretism handed down within the Shingon sect, which involved the identification of *kami* with Buddhas. For example, the monk Shōnin was interested in Mount Omiwa, and drew up a theory whereby the *kami* of Omiwa was identified with Mahāvairocana (Dainichi).[19]

Kūkai established an important monastic complex on the holy mountain of Kōyasan (Mount Kōya) in Kii province. Kōyasan resembles Mount Hiei in most aspects except for one: its close association with death. There is only one grave on Mount Hiei, that of Saichō himself, while the approach to Kōbō Daishi's tomb on Kōyasan is lined by tens of thousands of graves and mausoleums. To walk past them is a fascinating experience, the litany of the names of those buried therein reading like a catalogue of the greatest figures from Japanese history. There one may find the tomb of Akechi Mitsuhide, the usurper of the great Oda Nobunaga in 1582, whose monument was suitably blasted by a thunderbolt as a warning to faithless retainers. The custom of being buried on Kōyasan dates back to the 12th century and is directly related to the cult that developed around Kōbō Daishi following his death. According to Shingon belief, Kōbō Daishi did not die, but sits in a trance in his tomb

One of the many tombs and mausoleums of Japan's *daimyō* that are to be found on the holy mountain of Kōyasan. The custom of being buried on Kōyasan dates back to the 12th century and is directly related to the cult that developed around Kōbō Daishi following his death.

40

on Kōyasan awaiting the advent of Maitreya (Miroku Bosatsu), the Buddha of the Future. Such beliefs led to the desire for a spiritual bond with the 'saint' (no other word adequately conveys the respect and love in which Kōbō Daishi is held) by having one's remains, even a lock of one's hair, buried in this holy place. Failing this, a simple monument like a mausoleum would have to suffice.

That, at any rate, is the pious view. Others see in the tombs of the *daimyō* (independent warlords) on Kōyasan, some of which now appear to be at dangerous risk of collapse, a 'competition to overawe people with displays of magnificence'.[20] Kōyasan, a place of pilgrimage, provided too much of a temptation to show off, but its sacred nature has ensured its survival over the centuries in spite of a succession of samurai commanders who plotted its destruction in revenge for sanctuary given to a rival. Toyotomi Hideyoshi came the nearest to attacking Kōyasan after its denizens had supported his rival, Tokugawa Ieyasu (1542–1616), during the 1584 Komaki campaign, but his reverence for the holy mountain of Kōbō Daishi stayed his hand. Hideyoshi's connection with the place is better known through an anecdote concerning a visit he made after completing the reunification of Japan. According to legend, the third and final bridge along the avenue leading to Kōbō Daishi's tomb cannot be crossed by anyone whose morals are unacceptable to the saint. When Hideyoshi arrived he strode across the bridge in a confident manner that befitted his exalted state. What no one except the sympathetic abbot of Kōyasan knew was that Hideyoshi had made a trial crossing of the bridge the previous night, when nothing untoward had occurred.[21]

Kōyasan also played a key role throughout samurai history as a place of exile. A disgraced or defeated general might be allowed to shave his head and become a monk as a merciful alternative to committing suicide. Such generosity was usually accompanied by the wretch's banishment to a distant island, but Kōyasan provided a workable alternative. Unlike death, of course, exile to Kōyasan still left open the possibility of the victim's return. After the battle of Sekigahara in 1600, Sanada Yukimura was compelled to shave his head and become a monk on Kōyasan. He was still there when Toyotomi Hideyori's call to arms was issued in 1614. Yukimura escaped and joined in a final attempt to challenge the Tokugawa at the siege of Osaka castle while his brother Nobuyuki fought in the siege lines against him. But if Kōyasan did not provide a secure prison, neither did it offer a complete guarantee of sanctuary. Toyotomi Hidetsugu, originally chosen as Hideyoshi's heir, was banished to Kōyasan on the suspicion of treasonable conduct. This was very largely because Hidetsugu now stood in the way of Hideyoshi's infant son Hideyori. Mindful that Hidetsugu might leave the mountain and foment a genuine rebellion, Hideyoshi sent orders for him to commit suicide, and Hidetsugu had no option but to comply.[22]

THE EVE OF DESTRUCTION

The above accounts of holy men doing holy things on holy mountains may have given the impression that the Heian Period was living up to its name and promising peace to all. But as the centuries wore on after the passing of Saichō and Kūkai a new feeling of pessimism descended, prompted by certain gloomy mathematical calculations. Quite early in its history Buddhism had developed the concept of the three periods of the Buddhist Law. The period in which the teachings of Sākyamuni Buddha were transmitted faithfully was known as the

A statue of Jizō stands in front of a rather precarious-looking stone pagoda among the tombs that surround Kōbō Daishi's last resting place on Kōyasan.

period of Righteous Law (*shōbō*). The age of decline, in which enlightenment was no longer possible, was known as the period of Counterfeit Law (*zōbō*). Finally, the end of the Law, the time in which neither practice nor attainment wash possible, was known as the period of Decay of the Law (*mappō*), when the world would descend into chaos, darkness and destruction. The first two ages would last for a thousand years each, so the Japanese reckoned that the first millennium had been encompassed between the time of the life of the historical Buddha in around 500 BC and the introduction of Buddhism to Japan in AD 552. Simple arithmetic therefore indicated that in about the year 1052 the world would enter upon the awful time of *mappō*.[23] To Fujiwara Sukefusa (1007–57) the significance of that terrible year was proved beyond any doubt when fire destroyed the Hasedera temple.[24] To this awesome date was juxtaposed the concept of *mujō* (the impermanence of all phenomena), which enshrined the second of Buddhism's 'Four Noble Truths': that people suffer because they desire to possess things, even though nothing can be truly possessed because everything is impermanent and transient.

The acceptance of *mappō* and *mujō* had several important outcomes, not the least of which was the establishment of the Pure Land sects described later in 'Warriors of the Pure Land'. One could also put one's faith in Miroku, the Buddha of the Future. This gave hope to mankind even in the age of *mappō*, and some saw optimistic signs in the world about them. Fujiwara Munetada (1062–1141) noted that thieves who robbed a temple in 1096 were moved by dreams to return all the stolen property.[25] A very different manifestation in Japanese Buddhism, however, seemed to provide the evidence that the 'last days' had indeed arrived. With the steady rise in influence of the samurai class at the expense of the Chinese-inspired bureaucracy of the imperial court, factions within Buddhism itself degenerated into violent confrontation and wielded armies of *sōhei*, who are usually referred to as 'the warrior monks'.

There was no inherent reason why political disagreements over the affairs of important religious institutions should necessarily lead to armed conflict; however, by the middle of the 10th century bitter disputes over imperial control of senior appointments led to brawling between rival monks and eventually to the use of weapons. These inter-temple or inter-faction disputes were not 'religious wars' in the Western sense: they did not involve points of doctrine or dogma, just temple politics. The first major incident in 949 involving violence by monks against monks occurred when 56 monks from Nara's Tōdaiji gathered at the residence of an official in Kyōto to protest against an appointment that had displeased them. One important characteristic of such incursions was the carrying of religious symbols, a dramatic feature that underlined the complete sympathy between Shintō and Buddhism at that time. The Kōfukuji *sōhei* would carry at the head of their processions the *shimboku* (holy tree) of the Kasuga shrine, while the Mount Hiei monks carried the *mikoshi* – the portable shrines

A samurai prays at the entrance to a Shintō shrine at Mishima. From a woodblock printed book of 1835 by Hokkei, a pupil of Hokusai, depicting a journey from Edo to Kyōto.

seen today in shrine festivals – belonging to the Hiyoshi shrine at the foot of Mount Hiei.

In 969 a dispute over conflicting claims to temple lands resulted in the death of several Kōfukuji monks at the hands of monks from Tōdaiji. Also around this time we read of Enryakuji being involved in a dispute with the Gion shrine in Kyōto and using force to settle the matter. Subsequent to this incident Ryōgen, the chief abbot of Enryakuji, decided to maintain a permanent fighting force on Mount Hiei. His dramatic decision was contrary to both the letter and the spirit of the pronouncements he had made previously regarding monastic discipline. He had issued a code of 26 articles intended to curb widespread abuses by the clergy of Mount Hiei. These included rules that forbade monks from carrying weapons, inflicting corporal punishment or violently disrupting religious services.

Trouble started in 1039 when the incumbent abbot of Enryakuji's daughter temple of Miidera (Onjōji) was appointed abbot of Enryakuji. The two temples did not see eye to eye, so 3,000 enraged monks from Mount Hiei poured into Kyōto and descended on the residence of Fujiwara Yorimichi. When he refused to alter his decision, his gates were kicked in. The terrified official summoned the samurai to restore order, resulting in a bloody fight. Ultimately, violence and intimidation prevailed, because Yorimichi gave in and named the Mount Hiei candidate as abbot instead. The juxtaposition of these events with the supposed beginning of the age of *mappō* caused great concern. In 1037 the priests of Kōfukuji had attacked Tōdaiji and a certain Minamoto Norisato fought a battle against priests from the Iwashimizu shrine.[26] In 1074 and 1081 armies from Mount Hiei attacked Miidera. Miidera was attacked again in 1121 and 1141, and its buildings set on fire; henceforth, Miidera's hierarchy arranged for their novices to be ordained at Tōdaiji. When Enryakuji protested at this break from tradition, it was pointed out that Saichō, the founder of Enryakuji, had been ordained in Nara. This truthful comment so infuriated Mount Hiei that its warrior monks descended on Miidera and burnt it to the ground for the fourth time in a century.

Yet in spite of their intense rivalry and frequent conflicts, at times Enryakuji and Miidera were willing to join forces to attack a third party. Thus we hear of them united against Kōfukuji in 1081. In 1113 Enryakuji burned

the Kiyomizudera in Kyōto over a rival appointment of an abbot.[27] Enryakuji and Miidera united against Nara again in 1117 in an incident described in *Heike Monogatari*, the great epic of the 12th-century wars, which quotes the sad words of the ex-emperor Go Shirakawa-In: 'Three things refuse to obey my will: the waters of the Kamo River, the fall of backgammon dice, and the monks of Enryakuji Temple.'[28]

However, the monks could be controlled, as is illustrated by an incident at the north gate of Kyōto when the angry *sōhei* were confronted by the veteran samurai Minamoto Yorimasa. Yorimasa first won the confidence of the monks by quickly dismounting from his horse, taking off his helmet, rinsing his mouth with water and bowing to the *kami* of Sannō. His men immediately followed his example. In a brilliant display of diplomacy, Yorimasa then persuaded the monks not to attack the north gate, explaining that it was but lightly defended, and to force their way in would make the monks a laughing stock. Secondly, even though Yorimasa had been ordered to hold the gate by imperial command, as someone who respected the *kami* he could not oppose the monks' progress, and would have to abandon the way of the warrior. Thus persuaded, the Mount Hiei army moved to the eastern gate, where they were greeted not by a respectful commander but by a hail of arrows, some of which struck the sacred *mikoshi*. Partly as a reaction to this unprecedented act of sacrilege, and partly because of the strong resistance, the warrior monks retreated, leaving the *mikoshi* at the gate.

The five-storey pagoda of the temple of Kōfukuji in Nara, looking across from the pool of Sarusawa. The original pagoda was built in 725, and this one dates from 1426. It is the second tallest pagoda in Japan. The pool of Sarusawa appears in several accounts of the warrior monk battles that took place in Nara.

The Tōkondō or Eastern Golden Hall of the warrior monk temple of Kōfukuji in Nara. The original structure was built in 726 and was burned during the Gempei War. The present building was erected in 1415.

This incident has sometimes been portrayed as an example of the contrast in attitude between the 'superstitious' courtiers on the one hand and agnostic samurai on the other. But this is to view the situation through the biased eyes of the compilers of *Heike Monogatari*, whose monastic authors looked back on the conflict through a Buddhist lens and saw the eventual defeat of the Taira family as punishment for sins against Buddhism. In reality the samurai respected the sacred as much as the courtiers did, and within days the six men whose arrows had hit the *mikoshi* were identified and imprisoned.[29]

The activities of the soldier priests of the ancient Shintō establishments are less well known than those of the two major Buddhist centres. In 1082 *sōhei* of the Kumano shrine entered Kyōto with their *mikoshi* to protest about the murder of one of their number by an official. They returned in 1104 and rioted in Uji that same year. Just as in the case of samurai families, the *sōhei's* belligerence could be made to serve the court's ends. In 1114 the chief priest of Kumano was commissioned to pursue and capture the pirates who infested the coastline of Kii province.[30]

In 1180 the warrior monks became directly involved in the tragic civil war that was about to begin. The conflict, which lasted from 1180 to 1185, is known as the Gempei War because of the Chinese readings of the names of the two main protagonists: the Minamoto family (Gen) and the Taira (Hei). Prince Mochihito, the candidate for the imperial throne who was favoured by the Minamoto family, raised the standard of revolt in a proclamation couched as much in religious terms as political ones:

The wonderful Great Buddha of Nara inside the Daibutsuden of Tōdaiji. The original dated from 745–49, and was then recast twice after the first one was destroyed in 1181. It weighs 550 tonnes and is made from an alloy of bronze, mercury and fine gold.

[the Taira] have despoiled the graves of princes and cut off the head of one, defied the emperor and destroyed Buddhist law in a manner unprecedented in history... If the temporal rulers, the Three Treasures and the native gods assist us in our efforts, all the people everywhere must likewise wish to assist us immediately.[31]

Mochihito received a positive response from the veteran Minamoto Yorimasa, but his efforts were negated by a swift response from the Taira, who drove his supporters out of Kyōto. Along with monk allies from Miidera the retreating army decided to make a stand at the Uji river south of Kyōto, where they hoped to hold back the advancing Taira until warrior monks from Nara could move up to assist them. The Minamoto and their monk allies were subsequently defeated in a fierce battle across the broken Uji Bridge, and terrible retribution followed. First, Miidera was attacked and burned to the ground, the smoke from its smouldering buildings sending a warning to the Enryakuji high above it on Mount Hiei. Yet, as in so many cases in Japanese history, rebuilding began almost immediately. Japanese temples, being made all from wood, were no strangers to fire, and by 1183 it is recorded that monks from Miidera opposed the occupation of Kyōto by Minamoto Yoshinaka, so it must have been restored by that date.[32]

In 1181 the Kumano *sōhei* went to war again, and when a counter-attack was launched against them the *sōhei* took 30 people hostage, including women and children.[33] The compiler of *Azuma Kagami*, however, sympathized with the monks because they were fighting against the Taira family who had dared to impose a rice tax on families located around the Great Shrine of Ise – an unparalleled insult to Amaterasu.[34] The Taira took their revenge, and so fierce was the attack that some of the Kumano priests defected to their side. Others followed a few years later and fought at the battle of Dannoura in 1185, their change of allegiance resulting from an oracle received from the *kami* enshrined at Kumano.[35]

The Taira attack on the Kumano *sōhei* was a very minor operation compared to an event during that same year of 1181, when Taira Shigehira led a punitive expedition against Nara in retaliation for its support of Prince Mochihito. Unlike Miidera, the loss was significant and was not so easily repaired. The warrior monks put up a stiff resistance, which Shigehira overcame by using the indiscriminate weapon of fire. It may have been an accident that the fire spread so far, but the whole of the Tōdaiji complex disappeared in the flames, including Emperor Shōmu's Great Buddha, which melted in the intense heat. The burning of Nara was the greatest deliberate destruction of the material culture of Japanese Buddhism that the country was to witness in almost a thousand years, and the flames indicated the arrival of *mappō* in no uncertain terms. It was a crime that shocked heaven itself:

> How must the Four Deva Kings, the Eight Dragon Sea-gods, and the Judges and Custodians of the Underworld have been struck with amazement, and what must have been the concern of Kasuga Daimyōjin, the Tutelary Deity of the Fujiwara house? Even the dew on Mount Kasuga changed its hue and the wind howled mournfully on Mount Mikasa.[36]

This quotation is from *Heike Monogatari*. In the context of deep Buddhist pessimism derived from the concept of *mappō*, the progress of the Gempei War is seen in this work as the remorseless working out of karma, which itself reflects a belief in *mujō* – the impermanence of everything. The tone is set by its opening paragraph, one of the most famous passages in Japanese literature:

> The sound of the bell of Gionshoja echoes the impermanence of all things. The hue
> of the flower of the teak tree declares that they who flourish must be brought low.
> Yea, the proud ones are but for a moment, like an evening dream in springtime. The
> mighty are destroyed at the last, they are but as the dust before the wind.[37]

The statue of 'Hoichi the Earless', the blind *biwa* player who was renowned for his chanting of *Heike Monogatari*, the epic story of the destruction of the Taira family. The statue is at the Akamagu shrine near Shimonoseki, the site of the battle of Dannoura in 1185, where the Taira were finally defeated.

日本名將鑑

こゝに氏光が子上野の庄司
元弘の亂ふたゝび大塔宮の音
舍弟義助と謀り同二年
倉太刀を流
由比ヶ
潟きを
北條高時と
足利尊氏と戰ひ越前の
流矢に當りて沒す享三五七

THE GODS GO TO WAR

Few passages in the *gunkimono* (war tales) of Japan elicit a chuckle. With their concentration on the inevitable working out of remorseless fate against a background of the degenerate age of Buddhism, there is not much space for humour. One exception, albeit unintentionally, occurs in *Taiheiki*, the epic chronicle of the 14th-century civil wars, when a reverse during the siege of Chihaya is attributed to, of all things, the losing side's inability to write decent poetry:

> Now when the fighting was stopped, the warriors' spirits were wearied beyond endurance by lack of occupation. They brought down linked verse teachers of the Hana-no-mono school from the capital and began a linked verse of ten thousand stanzas, whereof the opening stanza on the first day was composed by Nagasaki Kurō Saemon-no-jō: 'Forestalling the rest, show your triumphant colours, O wild cherry!' Kudō Uemon-no-jō added a supporting stanza: 'The tempest indeed will prove the blossoms' foe.' To be sure, the words of both these stanzas were skilfully allusive; likewise the form was superior. But was it not auspicious to call their own side blossoms and compare the enemy to a tempest? So indeed it was later understood.[1]

The account goes on to say that in addition to poetry contests, games of backgammon and tea-judging helped pass the boredom of the siege. These, presumably, had less deleterious effects upon its subsequent outcome, because poetry, unlike backgammon, was very closely linked to prayer, and its composition could be seen as a prayerful act. In this sense it was merely one rather elaborate way whereby intercession with the *kami* might be carried out.

Of all the *kami* the ones more likely than others to be addressed by samurai were the 'gods of war'. Hachiman is often referred to as *the* god of war, but even though his name was frequently invoked there were others. The list included three Buddhist deities (Marishiten, Daikokuten and Benzaiten); three Shintō *kami* from ancient mythology (Takemikazuchi, Futsumeshi mikoto and Kashima Daimyōjin); and historical or semi-historical personages who had been deified, such as Hachiman, his mother Empress Jingū, Takeuchi sukune, and, very surprisingly, Prince Shōtoku, Nara Buddhism's greatest spokesman. If there was any confusion over the gods' identities rituals might simply be offered to 'the 98,000 gods of war'.[2]

The gods of war may have demonstrated their displeasure from time to time – defeat in battle was a sure sign of this – but steps could be always taken to avoid such a tragedy. Descriptions of Japan's early military expeditions are scarce, but an operation in 602 against the Korean kingdom of Silla provides a fascinating glimpse into the early relationship between the world of the warrior and the world of the *kami*. When Prince Kume set off for Korea his army included Shintō priests, who offered prayers for victory and blessed weapons before battle. Prince Kume would have taken part in these rituals.[3]

On occasion, the war gods made it clear that they were actually pleased as a result of some action carried out by a sentient being. When Ashikaga Takauji (1305–58), the first Shogun of the Ashikaga Dynasty, advanced on Kyōto in 1336 he observed a pair of doves fluttering above his white banner. This was a highly auspicious omen, as doves were regarded as the symbol of Hachiman: their arrival at the head of Takauji's army assured Hachiman's favour. The

The interior of the Isaniwa Hachiman shrine in Dōgo Onsen near Matsuyama, showing the votive offerings in the form of doves, the messengers of Hachiman. If a clan that was devoted to Hachiman saw doves on the way to battle it was a very good omen.

Taiheiki adds that the apparition also caused thousands of enemy troops to desert to the cause of the highly favoured Ashikaga.[4] During the same campaign, Takauji composed verses in honour of Kannon, the Goddess of Mercy. Shortly afterwards he had a dream in which her image appeared in a brilliant light on the bow of his ship, accompanied by 28 attendant deities, each fully armed. The favourable wind that ensued was attributed to Kannon's favour, just as Takauji's contemporary Imagawa Ryōshun was to do when a similarly favourable wind rewarded his poetic efforts. '[These events] could only indicate the actions of the gods,' he wrote. 'My foolish poems moved [them].'[5]

SERVANT OF HACHIMAN

Poetry and prayers immediately before a battle were only a small part of a general's spiritual preparations. To be absolutely successful the religious groundwork had to be laid much earlier. In 1180 the future Shogun Minamoto Yoritomo (1147–99) was in Izu province when he received the proclamation of Prince Mochihito. The later *Heike Monogatari* account depicts him as reluctant to respond, having to be goaded into action by the priest Mongaku, who presents Yoritomo with the skull of his father Yoshitomo, slain by the Taira.[6] The *Azuma Kagami* reports no delay other than that of religious obligation. Yoritomo's first act, before even opening the document that launched the Gempei War, was to don ceremonial robes and bow in the direction of the Iwashimizu Hachiman shrine, just as Matsuura Shigenobu was to do hundreds of years later. By this act he entrusted the fortunes of the Minamoto cause to their tutelary *kami*.[7]

Yoritomo was a child of his times, and a few months later he directs other prayers towards the Buddhist pantheon. Attempting to recite one thousand passages from the Lotus Sutra, he has trouble reaching his target; however, a Buddhist priest versed in numerology reassures him. He points out that as Yoritomo is the follower of Hachiman, whose name literally means 'eight banners', and the descendant of Hachiman Tarō Yoshiie, the great Minamoto hero, and because he was also the man chosen to punish the eight crimes of the Taira leader Kiyomori, whose residence in Kyōto was on Hachijō (Eighth Avenue), then 800 passages would suffice.[8]

Yoritomo's religious preparations continued with the recruitment of two useful volunteers to his flag. One was a samurai who was 'deeply versed in Shintō ritual', while the other was a Shintō priest who claimed descent from a priest attached to the Great Shrine of Ise. Yoritomo took them into his service so that they might conduct prayers on his behalf. Even though the former was a samurai and would therefore be expected to fight, the religious contribution he could make was valued more highly.[9]

The priest Mongaku goads Yoritomo into rebellion by showing him the skull of his father, Minamoto Yoshitomo, who was murdered by the Taira.

The first service that Yoritomo's new recruits performed was an act of divination to determine the best day to launch his attack. This reflected very ancient beliefs linked to Taoism, introduced from China in the 7th century AD. Spanning a wide system of belief and practices, Taoism incorporates divination and geomancy, and is expressed through notions of lucky directions, lucky days and years, and a wide range of complex taboos. In Japanese history Taoism has never stood alone as a separate religious system, but has been thoroughly mixed with Buddhism and Shintō. For centuries it has been an indirect but persuasive influence, incorporating many elements otherwise identified as 'folk practice'.

Taoism involved the religious principles of *onmyōdō* (the way of yin and yang). The Chinese term yin-yang refers to the two complementary forces of the universe that must balance each other to ensure harmony. Yin is the principle of darkness, cold and femininity. Yang is the principle of brightness, heat and masculinity; their interaction produces the five elements of wood, fire, earth, metal and water. A government bureau of religious Taoism was established as early as AD 675, its greatest achievement being the introduction to Japan of the Chinese lunar calendar, which was based on Taoist principles. Its influence extended far beyond the delineation of festival days to the identification of certain times as being intrinsically lucky or unlucky. For example, a journey should not be started on the eighth day of the month, and rice should not be planted on the day of the Sign of the Horse. Cloth for making clothes is best cut on the Day of the Rabbit, but no laundry should be done on the 15th or 28th days. There was also a list of inauspicious dates to

Minamoto Yoritomo, the first permanent Shogun of Japan, was typical of his age in that he had a firm belief in the influence of the *kami* on the outcome of a battle.

avoid for setting out to war, which included festival days. Certain places were also luckier than others, and warriors would invariably launch rebellions from within shrine precincts rather than from within temples.[10]

Yoritomo's new recruits worked out the best date for his attack, but by the eve of the appointed day, when more prayers for victory were being offered, an important contingent of the Minamoto army had not yet arrived. Yoritomo's greatest concern was that postponing the attack would impinge on a very important Buddhist ceremony scheduled for the next day. In the event, the missing samurai arrived during the early afternoon of the planned day, so Yoritomo's initial move against the Taira – a comparatively minor skirmish – took the form of a night attack. Although the assault was entirely successful, Yoritomo now had fresh religious concerns: he feared that his military campaigning would prevent him from purifying himself through his daily recitation of the Buddhist sutras. His solution was to find a nun who would do them on his behalf, much to the relief of all concerned.[11] The final religious act of this military operation was a promise to make good the damage done to certain temple lands by his campaigning warriors.[12]

So far Yoritomo's religious life was probably not atypical of the samurai class as a whole. He accepted Shintō and Buddhism as being basically the same and showed great concern over matters of divination and good luck, although there was a certain ritualistic element involved in the interpretation of omens as lucky or unlucky. For example, if a samurai was thrown by his horse when preparing for war, it was an unlucky omen only if he fell off on the right-hand side; a fall to the left was considered lucky. Similarly, if he had the misfortune to break his bow, it was an unlucky omen only if the bow broke below the hand grip. If the horse turned naturally towards the direction of the enemy, that was considered good luck; it was bad luck if the horse turned towards the general's own troops.

Certain actions thought likely to bring bad luck were avoided prior to battle. Many involved Shintō notions of ritual purity, the most polluting elements being contact with blood, birth or death. Sexual intercourse before going on campaign was absolutely forbidden, and a general had to ensure that none of his clothes or equipment came into contact with a pregnant woman. In a similar vein, no samurai setting off to war was to come into contact with a woman within 33 days of her having given birth, or with a woman having her menstrual period. Taoist notions of lucky direction further forbade a samurai from placing his suit of armour in a north-facing direction.

It is also interesting to discover that Yoritomo wore religious amulets. One was a *juzu*, a string of prayer beads similar to a Catholic rosary. Yoritomo was to lose it during the subsequent battle of Ishibashiyama, and was overjoyed when it was brought to him after his flight from the battlefield.[13] The *Azuma Kagami* notes that the *juzu* was well known to his companions. The other item was a tiny statuette of Kannon, the Goddess of Mercy, which he had worn in his pigtail since childhood.[14] Yoritomo removed the image prior to the battle and hid it in a cave, explaining that this was not so much because he was afraid of losing the treasured amulet, but that if his head were cut off he would be ridiculed for having an image in his hair. Clearly, the demands of personal religious devotion were not universally respected.[15]

Despite Yoritomo's thorough preparation, the gods did not smile upon him when he was defeated in his first major encounter with the Taira at the battle of Ishibashiyama. He wisely decided to regroup and set up his headquarters in the little seaside town of Kamakura. In part the location was chosen for sound political reasons. Kamakura was a safe distance from imperial Kyōto, which was dominated by the Taira, and it was also close to the traditional Minamoto heartlands. The choice of Kamakura had considerable religious significance as well. It was the site of the important Tsurugaoka Hachiman shrine, the foremost centre in eastern Japan for the worship of the *kami* who was the Minamoto family's tutelary deity.

The historical blending of Shintō and Buddhism is shown by the inclusion of this Inari shrine within the courtyard of the Buddhist temple of Kiyomizudera in Kyōto. To the left is seen a rack laden with *ema* – painted votive offerings bearing handwritten prayers.

The Kamakura Tsurugaoka Hachiman shrine dated from 1063, when Yoritomo's ancestor Minamoto Yoriyoshi (995–1082) had established it in gratitude for his victory in the so-called 'Former Nine Years' War'. It was probably through his guard duties in the capital that Yoriyoshi first became attached to Hachiman, who was prominently enshrined at the Iwashimizu Hachiman shrine to the south of Kyōto. In founding another shrine in Kamakura, Yoriyoshi welcomed this powerful *kami* to the general area of his military triumphs. His ambitious descendant, Minamoto Yoritomo, entered Kamakura in 1180, and on the morning after his arrival he made a visit to the Hachiman shrine. Yoritomo had plans for Kamakura, which included relocating the shrine, but it was first necessary to seek the *kami*'s approval for such a radical act. So Yoritomo purified himself by abstinence from meat and drew lots at the shrine's altar. The decision was a favourable one.[16]

The *Azuma Kagami* goes on to record Yoritomo's personal visits to the Hachiman shrine, detailing his determination to use its rebuilding and patronage as a symbol of his role as the head of the Minamoto family. As the religious focus of his campaign against the Taira, the Tsurugaoka Hachiman shrine remains today as a potent reminder of the power of the Minamoto, even though it is somewhat changed in form from its early role. At the time of the Gempei War it was a prime example of a *jingū-ji* (shrine/temple) complex, a product of the blending of Shintō and Buddhism that had characterized the Heian Period. Today, as a result of the separation of Buddhism and Shintō enforced by the Meiji government in the late 19th century, no traces of its once vibrant Buddhist nature remains.[17]

Not slow to recognize the honour that Yoritomo had done to him, Hachiman blessed him with his first victory against the Taira at the battle of the Fujigawa, where the Taira samurai were alarmed into thinking that the noise made by a flock of wildfowl was a surprise night attack.[18] It was a turning point in the Gempei War. From this time on, Yoritomo took almost no part in the actual fighting and left the business of defeating the Taira to his brothers Yoshitsune and Noriyori and his cousin Yoshinaka. This was accomplished through major victories at Kurikara (1183), Ichinotani (1184) and Yashima (1184). Even before Yoritomo's 'crowning mercy' that was the battle of Dannoura in 1185 – a naval battle where the sea ran red with the blood of the Taira and the red dye from their flags – he had sufficient confidence in his ultimate triumph to pledge his support for the righting of a great wrong:

> Regarding the Tōdaiji: the aforementioned temple has been damaged by Heike rebels, and subjected to the trials of a fire. Its images have been burned to ashes and its priests and monks have perished. Rarely has a temple seen such trials and tribulations, for which I express my personal grief. I now pledge the repair and reconstruction of this temple so that it might continue to offer prayers for the defence and safety of the nation. Although the world is in decline, the benign virtue of the ruler will promote the prosperity of both the imperial government and the Buddhist Law.[19]

The Tsurugaoka Hachiman shrine in Kamakura, founded by Minamoto Yoriyoshi to enshrine the tutelary deity of the Minamoto family. Yoritomo used the shrine as the focus of his efforts to build a power base in eastern Japan.

Yoritomo's final victory at Dannoura eliminated Taira influence and established Yoritomo as Japan's first permanent Shogun. The victory was remarkable in many ways, not least for the Taira's extraordinary decision to take with them into battle the infant Emperor Antoku and the three sacred emblems that made up the Japanese crown jewels. When the battle was lost the young emperor's grandmother jumped into the sea with the child, drowning them both. 'Ah, the pity of it,' says *Heike Monogatari* in its finest Buddhist rhetoric, 'That the gust of the spring wind of impermanence should so suddenly sweep away his flower form.'[20] The dowager empress had the sacred sword and the sacred jewel with her as she committed suicide. The jewel was recovered when the casket in which it was kept floated to the surface, but the sword was never found. Its disappearance was not lost on those who saw the signs of *mappō* all around them:[21] it was a warning that the imperial court had lost its vitality and would need to be defended by warriors, whose rise

山中鹿之助幸盛

芳年武者无類

Yamanaka Shika no suke, the loyal retainer of the Amako family, who prayed to the three-day-old moon for help in restoring the fortunes of the family.

to power was in itself indicative of the world's fallen state. This was the nearest that any Japanese person (in this specific case the monk Jien in his 13th-century history *Gukanshō*) could allow himself to move towards the Chinese notion of imperial rule by the mandate of heaven.[22]

With the coming of peace, Yoritomo found time to put other religious matters right. According to *Azuma Kagami*, since the death of his father

Yoshitomo in the Heiji insurrection of 1160, Yoritomo had read the Lotus Sutra every day to pray for the salvation of his parent's departed soul. In 1185 his wish to transfer his father's remains to Kamakura came true.[23]

The 'Kamakura Period' refers to the next 150 years of Japanese history, when the government passed from the imperial capital of Kyōto to Kamakura, the capital of the newly established *bakufu* or Shogunate. Even though the triumph of the Minamoto over the Taira was complete, they had only three generations left in which to enjoy the benevolence of the *kami*, and were in turn usurped by Yoritomo's widow's family, the Hōjō. Yet such was the respect for the institution of the Shogunate that the Hōjō ruled only as regents in the form of the Hōjō *shikken* until being overthrown in 1333. It was therefore under the rule of the Hōjō that the samurai and the sacred faced their most serious threat.

DIVINE INTERVENTION

By the middle of the 13th century the great Mongol Empire – begun by Genghis Khan and brought to its culmination by his grandson Khubilai Khan, the first Yuan (Mongol) emperor of China – had grown far beyond the grasslands of Central Asia. Japan first perceived a threat when the Mongols acquired control over Korea and its naval resources. In 1266 and again in 1269, Khubilai Khan sent envoys on a mission to Japan. The envoys reported back to Khubilai Khan that the Japanese were 'cruel and bloodthirsty' and lived in 'a country of thugs'.[24] This negative view may well have been one factor behind Khubilai Khan's decision to pacify the unruly island empire and bring it under his sway. Not surprisingly, his demand for tribute from Japan provoked a harsh reaction. The Japanese, who fully appreciated the threat of invasion thereby conveyed, were placed on their guard, and did not have to wait long for the outcome. Khubilai Khan gave orders to Korea to supply 900 ships and an army of 5,000 men. The fleet that finally set sail in 1274 included 15,000 Yuan (Mongol) soldiers and 8,000 Koreans, together with a very large number of crewmen.[25]

The Mongol invasions of Japan (Khubilai Khan's army returned in 1281) provided the only occasion in over 600 years when the samurai fought enemies other than themselves. The first attempt at invasion was a short-lasting affair, typical of the usual Mongol pattern of sending out a reconnaissance in force prior to a major campaign. It was met with incredible bravery by the samurai of the islands of Tsushima and Iki, and finally by the warriors of the mainland when the Mongols landed near Hakata in northern Kyūshū.

The Mongol invaders returned to Japan in 1281, determined to conquer and occupy the country, as evidenced by the inclusion of farm implements on board the invasion fleet.[26] Their vanguard attacked Tsushima and Iki, then attempted to land in Hakata Bay. As before, the ferocity of the Japanese defence

An *ema*, at the Isaniwa Hachiman shrine in Dōgo Onsen near Matsuyama, showing the action at the battle of Uji in 1184.

forced them back, but the Mongols established themselves on two islands in the bay. From there, they launched attacks against the Japanese for about a week, then withdrew offshore until reinforcements arrived. While the full fleet lay at anchor, a typhoon blew up and was devastating in its effects. Forced by the Japanese raids to stay in their ships and unable to drop anchor in protected harbour waters, the Mongol fleet was obliterated. Tens of thousands of men were left behind with the wreckage as the remains of the fleet headed home, and most of these were killed in Japanese attacks over the following few days. The typhoon became known as the *kami kaze* (divine wind), sent by the Sun-Goddess to aid her people.[27] It was this term, *kami kaze*, that the suicide pilots of World War II adopted as their title, thus identifying themselves with the successful destruction of an invader.

Decisive though the typhoon was, it would have been minimal in its effectiveness if the determination and fighting qualities of the samurai had not forced the entire fleet to lie at anchor with all their armies on board and unable to establish a beachhead. The samurai mounted their defence against a strange enemy that attacked in large formations and flung exploding bombs at them. When the dust had settled, all these factors had to be taken into account for the allotting of awards, a process that caused a strange and unique rift between the samurai and the sacred.

One outstanding example of an aggrieved samurai was Takezaki Suenaga. At the conclusion of hostilities, Suenaga felt that he had been denied the rewards that were properly his, so he took his complaints directly to the Hōjō's capital of Kamakura. His efforts to obtain a reward were every bit as insistent as his efforts against the Mongols, and of much longer duration. The journey to Kamakura from his home province of Higo took five months each way, with the interview lasting the better part of a whole day. He also commissioned a remarkable set of scroll paintings called the *Mōko Shūrai Ekotoba*.[28] The scrolls are among the most important primary sources for the appearance and behaviour of samurai in the 13th century, but they were never intended to be a historical document for posterity. They were instead created purely to press his claim for reward.[29] Suenaga eventually got what he wanted, even though his achievements were not quite as impressive as he seems to have thought. During the first invasion he did not kill a single Mongol. His sole achievement would appear to have been leading a suicidal charge with only four companions as the Mongols were retreating. His horse was killed under him, and Suenaga would almost certainly have been killed had another Japanese detachment not managed to rescue him. His military record in 1281 was better when he took part in one of the famous 'little ship' raids against the Mongol fleet. Using only his sword and his quick wits, Suenaga cut off some enemy heads.

The problem that Suenaga and his comrades faced lay in the two unique aspects of the Mongol campaign. The first was that, unlike any previous encounter since the birth of the samurai, there were no conquered enemy lands to share among the victor's faithful followers. The second problem was that in

An interesting trend in recent years in Japanese religion has been the erection of enormous statues of Kannon. This example is on the island of Ikitsuki, and from this angle its head appears to be poking out from the ground, although it is in a valley.

the distribution of largesse the samurai had to stand in line along with the sacred, because certain religious institutions pressed claims for reward every bit as insistently as those who had fought in battle. The basis for the claims lodged by shrines and temples was that their prayers had brought about the victory. The matter was not just concerned with the blowing of the *kami kaze*, which was commonly regarded as the answer to the prayers made at Ise to the Sun-Goddess by the representative of her earthly descendant. On other occasions during the fighting prayers had been made and had been answered appropriately. That the *bakufu* believed this is shown by the fact that at least two shrines, and possibly more, received rewards before any samurai did so. In addition, a letter of 1284 accompanying a donation to the Usa Hachiman shrine acknowledges the service rendered and asks the priest to keep praying, because 'it is rumoured that enemies may come to attack us again'.[30]

In commenting upon these claims it has been suggested that priests and monks 'made up stories which seem incredible to us today, giving the intervention of their deities full credit for the destruction of the Mongol armada in order to claim rewards'.[31] But this is to misunderstand the religious mindset of the times. Takezaki Suenaga fought, and he also prayed, as a belief in the 'this-worldly' efficacy of prayer permeated the whole of the samurai's environment. In the well-chosen words of Thomas Conlan, 'The battlefield was conceived as a realm where gods and buddhas mingled with men.'[32] Nevertheless, the resolution of the Mongol threat caused a temporary rift in this ancient acceptance. For the only time in Japanese history a dispute over reward placed the worlds of the samurai and the sacred into two separate and competing spheres in a way that would have been incomprehensible to Minamoto Yoritomo, whose personal victories were attributed to personal gods.

The actual situation regarding the claims for reward deposited by shrines and temples was a more extraordinary one than is implied by a simple fabrication of stories or competing claims by samurai and priests. In certain cases rival religious claims set *kami* against *kami*. In one extreme example, the Iwashimizu shrine claimed the credit for the raising of the *kami kaze* because of Buddhist prayers

The interior of the shrine on the island of Iki, dedicated to Taira Kagetaka, the governor of the island during the first Mongol invasion in 1274.

A dead samurai in full *yoroi* armour typical of the Kamakura Period wars, from the Kasuga Gongen Scroll.

that were offered on behalf of Hachiman, rather than that of Amaterasu. Seven hundred Buddhist monks had been involved in a seven-day-long service for the repulse of the Mongols, and Hachiman spoke through a medium to tell them that he had been so strengthened by prayer that he was about to blow the fleet away. A messenger later confirmed that this had occurred while the prayer service was in progress, and everyone was awestruck at the news.[33]

Monks and priests, whose petitions to the *bakufu* included reports of *kami* in the form of dragons, birds or monkeys, were as persistent as Takezaki Suenaga in seeking reward, and considerably more patient. As late as 1309 the chief priest of the Takeo shrine was to be found complaining that he still had received no reward, even though in 1274 the *kami* had shot arrows against the Mongol host, and in 1281 witnesses had seen three purple banners on top of his shrine flying towards the Mongol ships just before the *kami kaze* struck them.[34]

A PROPHET WITHOUT HONOUR

Among the new Buddhist sects that developed during the 13th century, Japan had acquired one that was to have a curious bearing on the religious side of the Mongol defeat. The monk Nichiren was born in 1222 in Awa province in eastern Japan. He entered the religious life, but finding that provincial Awa was not the best environment for his earnest and inquiring mind, he had studied on Mount Hiei. Unlike so many of his contemporaries, Nichiren did not become

A bas-relief on the plinth of a statue of Nichiren in Hakata. He is being escorted on his way to execution (a sentence later commuted) by armed samurai. The figure of Nichiren has been polished by the hands of numerous pilgrims.

the pupil of a particular teacher. Instead he found his inspiration among scripture, and soon became the greatest devotee of the Lotus Sutra.[35] To Nichiren this contained the essence and reality of all Buddhist teaching. To some extent, therefore, Nichiren did not turn away from the Tendai teaching, but turned back to it. He vehemently rejected the esoteric Buddhism that he felt had corrupted the original truths contained in the Lotus Sutra, where '*Namu Myōhō Renge-kyō!*' ('Hail to the Lotus of the Divine Law!') was the pledge of salvation, a phrase that could be easily and dramatically beaten in time with a drum.[36]

Nichiren did not believe that the disorder of the times was due to some cosmic arithmetic concerned with calculating the time of *mappō*. It was instead the inevitable consequence of a land that had abandoned the True Law and given itself over to false teachings. In 1260 he wrote *Risshō Ankoku Ron* (On Establishing the Correct Teaching and Pacifying the Nation), a religious polemic that he presented to the former regent of Japan, Hōjō Tokiyori. Tokiyori did not accept Nichiren's suggestion that natural calamities were the result of bad governance. This point came very near to political heresy, and in 1261 Nichiren was banished from Kamakura. He returned from a brief exile more belligerent than ever, and sustained a broken arm in a tussle with opponents.[37]

Nichiren gradually became more deeply entrenched in his views, demanding exclusive devotion to the Lotus Sutra. He called Kōbō Daishi 'the greatest liar in Japan'. The *nembutsu* (Buddha-calling) of the Pure Land sects was the cause of punishment in the lowest of hells, while Zen was the doctrine of demons.[38] These comments have naturally caused Nichiren and his followers to be accused

of having broken the tradition of religious tolerance in Japan,[39] although Nichiren's exclusivism was far more than mere intolerance.[40] By this time, the Japanese government had cause to take a new interest in this fiery outsider, because in his 1260 tract Nichiren had warned that unless Japan mended her ways she would be visited by the spectre of foreign invasion. The arrival of the Mongol envoys with Khubilai Khan's demands for tribute transformed Nichiren's image into that of a visionary. It was the period of greatest numerical growth among Nichiren's followers, but their harsh and uncompromising stand against all other believers made Nichiren into a prophet without honour in his own country. Harsh persecution followed and Nichiren was condemned to death, although the sentence was finally commuted to exile. On his way to execution the procession passed a shrine to Hachiman, where Nichiren stopped and mockingly challenged the great *kami* to save him.[41]

Nichiren kept his attitude of rigid exclusivity until his death in 1282, by which time the Mongols had come and gone. Unlike so many other religious figures who had been involved in some way with the tumultuous events of the Mongol invasions, Nichiren neither demanded nor expected any reward. His most tangible link with the Mongols exists today in the city of Hakata, where a memorial to the defeat of the invaders bears on its side scenes from the Mongol attacks and from his own life. Towering above them is a huge statue of the prophet, as fierce and uncompromising in bronze as he ever was in life; the perfect embodiment of Japan's most turbulent priest.

THE SACRED SAMURAI

It was not long before civil war began again, brought about by an attempt by Emperor Go Daigo to rule as his imperial ancestors had done before without the influence of a Shogun. In 1333 his supporters attacked the Hōjō capital of Kamakura, which was defended on three sides by mountains and on the fourth by the sea. In spite of hours of fierce fighting, no real breakthrough had been achieved by Nitta Yoshisada's investing army; however, he realized that there was a chance of outflanking the defences if it were possible to round the cape where the promontory of Inamuragasaki projects into the sea. There was a small expanse of beach at low tide, but the tide was high and the Hōjō had taken the added precaution of placing several ships a short distance from the shore, from which a barrage of arrows could cover any flanking attack.

Nitta Yoshisada resorted, quite naturally, to prayer. The words attributed to him in *Taiheiki* reflect exactly the religious belief of the times: the primacy of the founder of the imperial line whose cause Yoshisada had espoused and her identification with a supreme manifestation of Buddha, as well as the mysterious rule of the oceans by the dragon gods:

OPPOSITE

Katō Kiyomasa was a fervent adherent of the Nichiren sect, and is shown in this print in action at the battle of Shizugatake in 1583 with the Nichiren motto '*Namu Myōhō Renge-kyō!*' ('Hail to the Lotus of the Divine Law!') emblazoned on his *sashimono* (back flag).

The dying warrior.
A mortally wounded
samurai tries to rise
to his feet using his
blood stained sword.

I have heard that the Sun-Goddess of Ise, the founder of the land of Japan, conceals
her true being in the august image of Vairocana Buddha, and that she appeared in
this world in the guise of a dragon-god in the blue ocean. Now her descendant our
emperor drifts on the waves of the western seas, oppressed by rebellious subjects...
Let the eight dragon-gods of the inner and outer seas look upon my loyalty; let
them roll back the tides a myriad leagues distant to open a way for my host.[42]

So saying he took his sword and threw it into the sea as an offering to the
dragon-gods, and the waters parted like the Red Sea before Moses.

With the fall of Kamakura the reign of the Hōjō Regents, the family who
had defied the Mongols on Japan's behalf, came to an end. However, Go
Daigo's initial success faltered for the same reasons that had clouded the defeat
of the Mongols, when one of his followers, Ashikaga Takauji, felt that he had
not received sufficient rewards for his services. When the emperor sent him to
war again Takauji proclaimed himself as the new Shogun. This led to a long
conflict known as the Nanbokuchō War, the 'War Between the Courts' –

so called because the Ashikaga retaliated against their labelling as rebels against the throne by setting up their own nominee as emperor. Takauji also moved the Shogunate to Kyōto and established a palace in the Muromachi district of the city; thus, the time of Ashikaga rule is known as the Muromachi Period.

Just as Yoritomo was devoted to Kannon and carried an amulet of her with him, Ashikaga Takauji claimed to be particularly favoured by Jizō and carried with him a small statuette of this popular deity.[43] Jizō was originally the bodhisattva Ksitigarbha, whose worship may have appeared in Japan about the 10th century.[44] His particular role is to save those on their way to hell, and as a bodhisattva Jizō made a vow not to attain Buddhahood until the last soul in hell might be redeemed. Takauji's devotion to Jizō was somewhat unconventional for a member of the samurai class, since Jizō was seen more as the special protector of the lower classes in society. It is also interesting to see how this versatile Buddhist divinity took over the role of the traditional 'kami of the road', who was believed to guard the turning points of highways. Jizō added to this the concept of being the guardian of those who were at a turning point

in their lives, particularly those who were facing the life to come.[45] In the course of time Jizō also came to be regarded as the special protector of children who had died, including stillborn infants and aborted foetuses.[46] The combination of these two roles means that Jizō is one of the most common religious images seen in Japan today. Along with wayside Shintō shrines, it is the little stone statues of Jizō wearing babies' bibs and knitted woollen hats that most excite the curiosity of the visitor to Japan. They may be decorated with flowers or pinwheels, but the traditional votive offering to make before a Jizō is a pebble, because 'each of these pebbles meant one pebble less to be heaped up on the beach of the river in hell by the souls of the children, who stood under Jizō's protection'.[47]

Ashikaga Takauji's devotion to Jizō was of course very different, as the god guaranteed him military victory. Takauji repeatedly dreamed of Jizō, and also drew pictures of him. He may have hedged his bets with prayers and poetry to Kannon and Hachiman, but in a remarkable personal development Takauji believed that he was not only the unique recipient of Jizō's favour, but was

Nichiren's most tangible link with the Mongols exists today in the city of Hakata, where a memorial to the defeat of the invaders bears on its side scenes from the Mongol attacks and from his own life. Towering above them is a huge statue of the prophet, as fierce and uncompromising in bronze as he ever was in life; the perfect embodiment of Japan's most turbulent priest. This identical statue is in Kyōto.

Ashikaga Takauji was devoted to Jizō, shown here at Nara's Kōfukuji.

actually a manifestation of the bodhisattva on earth.[48] No samurai leader could go further than this in claiming divine guidance for his acts, and in fact none seem to have dared to make such an outrageous connection between god and man.

History was to record the gods' displeasure at this presumption, albeit mediated through the opinions of men. Although one of the most successful samurai commanders in Japanese history, Ashikaga Takauji is traditionally

reviled for opposing the cause of the rightful emperor Go Daigo and for bringing about the death in 1336 of Kusunoki Masashige: the nearest thing Japan ever produced to a samurai saint. Masashige, whose cult (there is no other adequate expression) was popularized during the Meiji Restoration when exemplars of loyalty towards the imperial ideal were sorely needed, met his end as a result of unquestioning devotion to the imperial will. Takauji, on the other hand, turned against the emperor and set up his own candidate for the throne. There is a wooden statue of him in the Tōji-In in Kyōto, and until recently one could pay a small fee to beat it with a stick. In such a way Ashikaga Takauji, the sacred samurai, suffered a long-delayed act of revenge from which neither Hachiman nor Kannon nor Jizō could save him.

A statue of Jizō surrounded by pebbles at Unzen, near Nagasaki. The pebbles have been left by visitors in the belief that this will help dead children in the afterlife.

WARRIORS OF THE PURE LAND

In the degenerate age of *mappō* one message of hope was embraced above all others: the reassurance provided by the *hongan* (original vow) of Amida Buddha not to attain Supreme Enlightenment so long as any human beings remained unsaved.[1] On their death the faithful would be taken to him in the western paradise of the Jōdo (Pure Land). Amidism, as this belief is known, took root in Japan by the mid-7th century, and was given a new prominence by the deep pessimism of the Heian Period.[2]

Pure Land Buddhism only became a separate sectarian entity with Hōnen's foundation of the Jōdo sect. Hōnen (1133–1212) studied on Mount Hiei, where the atmosphere in the mid-12th century was hardly conducive to quiet contemplation. The first Pure Land text that Hōnen read was *Ojō Yōshū* by the Pure Land pioneer Genshin, who stressed meditation on Amida as the best practice. Hōnen seriously questioned this point of view, believing that the time of *mappō* had begun and that ordinary people were sunk in a deep pit of suffering. Yet it was precisely for such an eventuality that Buddha had prepared the Pure Land path to salvation. But how many poor people, who were so much in need of salvation, could meditate? Tendai and Shingon may have possessed profound doctrinal systems and impressive esoteric rituals, but what good was the provision of a gateway to salvation if the majority of people could not hope to pass through it? Surely the recitation of Amida's name, an act of devotion that could be performed anywhere and under any conditions, was the true path to salvation? Thus it came about that the constant repetitive practice of *nembutsu* – the chanting of Amida's name through the invocation *Namu Amida Butsu* – became the centre of Jōdo devotion.[3]

OPPOSITE

Komizucha, a warrior monk from Negorodera in Kii province, a temple of the Shingi ('new meaning') branch of the Shingon sect. The monks of Negorodera fought alongside the Ikkō-ikki against Oda Nobunaga and were early converts to firearm technology. This print illustrates the final defeat of Negorodera by Toyotomi Hideyoshi in 1585.

THE TRUE PURE LAND

In about 1201 Hōnen had a visit from a monk from Mount Hiei called Shinran (1173–1262). After meditating for a hundred days Shinran had experienced a revelation: that rebirth in the Pure Land was assured at the moment one attained true faith in Amida, even if the person concerned was still in a state of sin. Shinran became one of Hōnen's keenest disciples, stressing the acceptance of two facts: the absolute power of Amida to save sinners, whom Shinran regarded as the principal object of Amida's compassion, and the absolute lack of power to achieve rebirth at the human level.[4] Where Shinran's teaching began to diverge from that of Hōnen lay in his attitude towards *nembutsu*, which Hōnen had understood as the chief way to salvation for the simple minds of people too weak to undertake the practice of meditation. Shinran saw *nembutsu* in a different light. The urge to pronounce the holy name was not a means toward achieving rebirth in the Pure Land but a gift from Amida. The inspiration to utter it came to the believer who knows that he is already saved. Therefore the constant repetition of the name was of no avail: salvation comes from Buddha and not from man. One single, sincere invocation would be

The Jōdo flag of Tokugawa Ieyasu, here split into two in a painted screen of the battle of Anegawa in 1570 in Fukui Prefectural Museum. It bears the slogan, 'Renounce this Filthy World and attain the Pure Land'.

enough, and any additional recitation of the holy name should be merely an expression of gratitude.

Shinran believed that ritual practices were a hindrance to true piety, not a help, writing in *Kyōgyōshinshō* that 'true faith inevitably provides the name, but the name does not assuredly provide the faith of the Vow Power'.[5] Also, because salvation comes from Buddha and not from the human person, a sinner can accept his own nature as it is. Sinful human beings therefore had the potential to attain salvation in this life in a state of enlightenment and were guaranteed rebirth in the Pure Land.[6] The similarities between these views and the teachings of Christ, who came 'not to call the righteous but sinners to repentance', would not be lost on the Jesuit missionaries to Japan, who labelled Shinran's Jōdo Shinshū (the True Pure Land sect) the 'Devil's Christianity'.

Hōnen and Shinran's approaches to Pure Land Buddhism, which contrasted sharply with the monastic approach of the older institutions, resulted in their banishment from Kyōto. Shinran's crime was that he had taken a wife in defiance of monastic discipline.[7] In 1272 Shinran's daughter Kakushin-ni (1221–81) built the Otani mausoleum in Kyōto to house the ashes of her father, and in 1321 Shinran's great-grandson Kakunyo (1270–1351) converted it into the first Honganji, the 'temple of the original vow'. Kakunyo developed Shinran's ideas into a coherent religious system, promoting the notion that Shinran was the founder of a sect. Up to that point Shinran's followers had been organized in scattered communities. From Kakunyo's time the expression 'Honganji' came to refer not only to the building that was its headquarters, but to the dominant faction in Jōdo Shinshū.[8]

Jōdo Shinshū shifted the emphasis of Japanese Buddhism from a monastic-centred organization to the ordinary lives of ordinary people for whom the practice of their religion was fundamental. Its teaching contrasted sharply with the older sects' insistence on the attainment of enlightenment through study, work or asceticism. Jōdo Shinshū welcomed all into its fold and did not insist upon meditation or intellectual superiority. To a Tendai monk Jōdo Shinshū belief was an illusory short cut to salvation. Yet, within Jōdo Shinshū, the consequences of non-belief could be dire. Excommunication was much feared within a religion-based community, and even execution could be threatened during times of war.[9] Jōdo Shinshū's inclusive nature was also reflected in its social organization. This included local membership centred around village meeting places, a charismatic leadership under the headship of Shinran's lineal descendants and a fundamental independence from traditional regimes, whether aristocratic or military.

The populist nature of the sect also led to changes in the architecture of its buildings. Orientation shifted from a south-facing *hondō* to one that looked towards the east, because Amida Buddha faces east from his western paradise. Other major changes came from the fact that Jōdo Shinshū temples were not

The vast interior of the Nishi Honganji in Kyōto is spacious enough for a large crowd of worshippers. The scale of the building reflects the enduring popularity of the sect.

monasteries but popular temples served by comparatively few priests. There were no cloistered corridors, lecture halls and pagodas. Nor do we see formal dormitory and refectory blocks. The quarters for the married priests were more like private houses, with gardens walled off from the public area. The most striking difference concerned the *hondō*. First, it was likely to be dedicated not to any conventional figure in the Buddhist pantheon but to Shinran Shonin as a *goeidō* (founder's hall). Second, a very common feature in the larger Jōdo Shinshū establishments was the existence of two main halls instead of just one. The second hall was dedicated to Amida and was smaller, although both were spacious enough for a large crowd of worshippers. Lamps twinkled on the pure gold surfaces of the altar furnishings. The air was heavy with incense and seemed to throb with the responses from hundreds of voices. To a believer the scene stood as a promise of the western paradise guaranteed by Amida Buddha, just as Shinran had intended.

THE AGE OF WARRING STATES

The second half of the 15th century was a time of great instability in Japan. Up to this time a remarkable consensus had provided an undercurrent of stability in Japanese society.[10] The imperial court nobility held the administrative and ceremonial responsibilities of the state. The samurai kept the peace and controlled turbulent members of its own class. The religious establishment, which was more diffuse and less coherent than the other two groups, supplied Japan with spiritual protection. None of the three could operate alone; nor did any of the three ever seek to eliminate either of the other two. Powers might be curtailed, and awkward individual rivals might be removed, but for four centuries the overall pattern was one of cooperation.[11]

During the 15th century this mutually supportive system began to break down. The Ashikaga had ruled Japan as Shoguns for over a century, but had become dominated by the petty quarrels of the *shugo*, the governors of a province or a group of provinces. The weakness of the Shogunate came to a disastrous climax with the outbreak of the Onin War in 1467. Kyōto was the main battleground, and by the time the fighting ended in 1477 most of the city lay in ruins. Though the original cause of the conflict had been a succession dispute within the Shogunate, by 1477 that had become irrelevant, with the Shogun rendered almost powerless to control the course of events. Worse still, the fighting had spread to the provinces as erstwhile *shugo* fought for supremacy and territory. Some succeeded in transforming themselves into independent lords, for which the term *daimyō* (literally 'great name') is used. But former *shugo* were not the only *daimyō*. Many *daimyō* were military opportunists who had seen their chances and created petty kingdoms of their own. Some hailed from ancient aristocratic families, but many seized power by usurpation, murder, war or marriage contracts to influential neighbours – indeed by any means that would safeguard their positions and their livelihoods. From chains of simple fortresses, *daimyō* controlled and guarded their provinces against optimistic tax collectors and pessimistic rivals. The period between 1467 and 1615 is known by analogy with Chinese history as the *Sengoku Jidai* (Age of Warring States).

Throughout this time, these rival warlords showed a strange respect for the supposed central rule of the Shogun, even though the later incumbents of the post depended for their survival on making alliances with them. In 1568 the post of Shogun was abolished altogether by Oda Nobunaga, the first of the three 'super-*daimyō*' who was to achieve the reunification of Japan. This proved to be only a temporary measure; the final unifier, Tokugawa Ieyasu, was of Minamoto descent, and became the first Tokugawa Shogun in 1603.

The rise of 'people power' through Jōdo Shinshū featured significantly in the period following the Onin War. Popular uprisings and riots became common, ranging from local disturbances to province-wide revolts. The latter were generally referred to as *ikki* (riots), the original use of the word that came to mean a league acting as a mutual protection association. Rennyo (1415–99), the eighth head of the Honganji and Jōdo Shinshū's great revivalist, created the greatest *ikki* of all: the Ikkō-ikki (single-minded league).[12] Their faith promising that paradise was the immediate reward for death in battle, the Ikkō-ikki *monto* (believers) welcomed fighting; nothing daunted them. When the Ikkō-ikki were about to go into battle, the sound of their mass *nembutsu* chanting chilled the blood of their enemies.

The creation of *ikki* alarmed the *daimyō* for reasons other than purely military ones – *ikki* formations cut right across the vertical vassal structures that they were trying to create. In some cases samurai retained membership of their *ikki* even after they became vassals of a *daimyō*. Weaning them away from such ties was very difficult if the *ikki* involved staunch religious beliefs such as were demanded by Jōdo Shinshū. A prime example is the situation that faced the young Tokugawa Ieyasu in the early 1560s. The Ikkō-ikki of Mikawa province were among his greatest rivals, but several of his retainers embraced Jōdo Shinshū. When issues of armed conflict arose, such men were placed in a quandary. For example, in the *Mikawa Go Fudoki* account of the battle of Azukizaka in 1564 we read the following:

> Tsuchiya Chokichi was of the *monto* faction, but when he saw his lord hard pressed he shouted to his companions, 'Our lord is in a critical position with his small band. I will not lift a spear against him, though I go to the most unpleasant sorts of hells!' and he turned against his own party and fought fiercely until he fell dead.[13]

The structure of an *ikki* was broadly democratic, and the visible proof that an agreement had been reached would take the form of a document. The signatures were often written in a circle to show the equal status of the members and to avoid quarrels over precedence. Next, a ritual was celebrated called *ichimi shinsui* (one taste of the gods' water), when the document was ceremoniously burned. Its ashes were mixed with water and the resulting concoction was drunk by the members. The ritual was thought to symbolize the members' like-mindedness that was the outward sign of their solidarity.

Similar democratic rules applied initially with the Ikkō-ikki, where oaths were signed on a paper that bore an image of Amida Buddha. As it developed, however, the structure of their organization became more hierarchical, with the ruling Honganji on top of the pyramid. Rennyo urged the *monto* to be prepared for unhesitating sacrifice in defence of their faith. Although he made it clear to his followers that resort to arms was justified only in the most extreme cases where the survival of Jōdo Shinshū was at stake, this was a radical departure from the original teachings of Shinran, but this was the Age of Warring States.

Unfortunately Rennyo's attitude made his organization open to possible abuse by militant *monto* who saw the ideological and military strength of the Honganji as a way of advancing their own interests. Rennyo soon became alarmed by the belligerence of some *monto* who attacked other sects and challenged the civil authorities. Membership also proved attractive for low-ranking members of the samurai class who were able to combine their own small forces under a common banner to produce an effective army. Rennyo viewed all samurai with distaste, writing that they were the 'enemies of Buddhism'; however, increasing numbers of samurai became *monto*. Their fighting skills were to prove useful in the years to come, most notably in the province of Kaga, where the Ikkō-ikki ousted the Togashi family and took over the province themselves. They ruled Kaga for the next hundred years. On one occasion they fought the powerful Uesugi Kenshin to a standstill, blocking his access to the capital. Not bad for a *hyakusho no motaru kuni* (province ruled by peasants), to use a popular phrase!

Rennyo retired in 1489, handing over the headship of the Honganji to his son Jitsunyo. In 1496, craving solitude, he built a hermitage on a sweeping bend in the Yodo river downstream from Kyōto. It lay on a long, sloping wooded plateau, and the 'long slope' gave the place its name: Osaka, the first documented use of the name of what is now Japan's second city. Osaka provided tranquillity for only a short time, however. Even in retirement, Rennyo commanded a huge and loyal following. Thousands flocked to pay homage to him, and by the time of his death in 1499 a new foundation called Ishiyama Honganji was beginning to take its final shape.

Rennyo (1415–99), the eighth head of the Honganji and Jōdo Shinshū's great revivalist. This painted hanging scroll is in the Yoshizakiji in Yoshizaki, where Rennyō exerted great influence.

The reality of samurai warfare, with its severed heads, is shown on this scroll in Ueda Castle Museum.

Ishiyama Honganji became the headquarters of the Ikkō-ikki after a dramatic incident in Kyōto, the location of Rennyo's former headquarters. By the early 16th century Kyōto had become the city of a rising urban class rebuilding their capital from the ashes of the Onin War. Most of these merchant families were adherents of the Nichiren sect. Jōdo Shinshū and Nichiren had much in common in terms of their defensive mentality, but were complete opposites when it came to recruitment. Jōdo Shinshū was largely drawn from peasants and country samurai, while Nichiren appealed to the townspeople. Kyōto had 21 Nichiren temples, and their members organized themselves by neighbourhoods for self-protection and mutual regulation.

During the 15th century spontaneous peasant mobs had frequently attacked the city. In the 1530s the Ikkō-ikki burned the Kōfukuji in Nara and ransacked the Kasuga shrine, causing considerable apprehension within Kyōto when it was rumoured that the capital was the next target. The Nichiren believers rallied round the flag of the Holy Lotus, and after some initial setbacks fought off an Ikkō-ikki assault. Much aggrieved, the Nichiren believers decided to hit back. Not lacking in sympathetic samurai allies, in 1532 they destroyed the Ikkō-ikki's Kyōto headquarters at Yamashina Midō.

The abandonment of Kyōto resulted in Ishiyama Honganji becoming the sect's headquarters for the next half century. Its strength was soon tested when

an army attacked in 1533. To the great relief of the Ikkō-ikki, their massive temple complex, set within a natural moat of rivers and sea, withstood the assault and indeed appeared to be impregnable. This welcome demonstration of its strength and safety encouraged further commercial settlement; the surrounding merchant community experienced considerable growth over the next few years. Ishiyama Honganji's wealth increased, and in 1536 the priests of the Honganji even paid all the expenses for the enthronement of Emperor Go Nara. It proved to be money well spent. In 1538 the leaders of Ishiyama Honganji negotiated a deal with the imperial court and the local military governor to make the surrounding merchant community into a *jinaimachi* (temple town), with immunity from debt moratoriums and from entry by outside military forces.

The self-contained community was such a success that by the middle of the 16th century a dozen or so smaller but similar *jinaimachi* had arisen in the provinces of Settsu, Kawachi and Izumi, which now make up the modern metropolitan district of Osaka. All of them were commercial and military strongpoints defended by walls and ditches, and each had obtained from the outside authorities a package of self-governing privileges. The days of the Ikkō-ikki as a simple rural peasant army had passed into history.

The Osaka communities benefited unexpectedly from the destruction of their Nichiren rivals in Kyōto. In 1536, by means of a raid of a type that the

The Goeidō mon (founder's gate) of Higashi Honganji, the present-day headquarters in Kyōto of the Otani branch of the Honganji, the 'original vow' temple of Jodō Shinshū. This immense gate was built in 1911.

81

city had not experienced for centuries, the warrior monks of Mount Hiei did the Ikkō-ikki's work for them. All 21 major temples of the Nichiren sect were burned to the ground, along with much of their surroundings. The *sōhei* spared the area round the imperial palace and the Shogun's headquarters, but the collateral damage was considerable.

In 1554 the leadership of the Honganji passed to Kennyo, who proved to be the most militant of all the Honganji leaders. The hour had come, and so had the man: Kennyo was soon to face the fiercest onslaught in all of the Honganji's history.

CHALLENGE TO THE HONGANJI

The 1560s and 1570s in Japan are dominated by the personality of one man: Oda Nobunaga (1534–82), who began the process of the reunification of Japan. As a brilliant and ruthless general, Nobunaga had begun his rise to power with a surprise victory at the battle of Okehazama in 1560. More success followed, and in 1568 he entered the capital to set up his nominee Ashikaga Yoshiaki as Shogun. Relations with Yoshiaki soon deteriorated and Oda Nobunaga dismissed him. The dispossessed Shogun sought allies elsewhere, including the Ikkō-ikki, who soon became Nobunaga's worst enemies.

The threat to Nobunaga from Ishiyama Honganji was not just a military one. It was also strategic and economic, with the power base of the Ikkō-ikki coinciding precisely with Nobunaga's own primary sphere of interest. The sect was particularly well entrenched within its fortified temples of Owari, Mino and Ise, the places where Nobunaga's own regime had been born. It lay across every approach to the capital save the west, from where the sympathetic *daimyō* Mōri Motonari (1497–1571) happily supplied them from his seaborne base. The creation of *jinaimachi* had lifted Jōdo Shinshū from its peasant roots into a position of economic power, so that Ishiyama Honganji could confront Nobunaga on commercial terms as well. He experienced his first armed clash with the Ikkō-ikki in 1570. Nobunaga was fighting Miyoshi Yoshitsugu near Osaka when forces from Ishiyama Honganji, including 3,000 men armed with arquebuses, reinforced the Miyoshi and caused Nobunaga to withdraw. Soon afterwards they struck a more personal blow when they forced his brother Oda Nobuoki to commit suicide at the siege of Ogie castle.

That same winter of 1570/71, when Nobunaga was driving back the Asai and Asakura armies in another campaign, his flank was attacked by *sōhei* from Enryakuji. Nobunaga must have thought that he was surrounded by religious fanatics, and when the time came to hit back he began with the nearest target: Mount Hiei, which had provided shelter for his enemies. In an operation so one-sided that it does not deserve the appellation of a battle, his troops moved against the *sōhei*. The samurai moved steadily up the mountain in an orgy of fire and slaughter, killing everyone and destroying everything in their way. The following accounts present opinions of the massacre from two opposing religious points of view. The first puts words into the mouths of those monks who did not beg to be spared by Nobunaga's samurai, but chose instead to cast themselves into the fires of the burning temple buildings:

> As the world, after the lapse of 550 years, has entered upon the period of the Latter Degenerate Days of the Law, there can be no hope for the future. If we burn together with the icons and the images of the Mountain king, the great Founder, and the Buddhas and Bodhisattvas, it may create for us the merit of attaining Buddhahood.[14]

Oda Nobunaga, who hated the Ikkō-ikki and supported the Christian missions because of their opposition to Buddhism. The fact that their gospel was one of opposition to Japanese religion *per se*, while Nobunaga was opposed merely to the use of it against him, was conveniently overlooked by the Jesuits.

By this time Jesuit missionaries were active in Japan, and Father Luis Frois concluded his own report of the events, written within days of them happening: 'Praise be to God's omnipotence and ultimate goodness, for he has ordered such a great hindrance to be punished with extinction, so that one day His holiest law will be propagated in these parts in abundance.'[15]

The destruction of Mount Hiei did not mean its end as a religious institution. The terrible message that Nobunaga had conveyed was that there was no equivalence between the samurai and the sacred, at least not when they were aimed at him. So, just as had happened in Nara after 1181, Enryakuji was rebuilt. The process cannot have taken too long, because in 1583, the 'marathon monk' Kōun completed a thousand-day *kaihyōgō* practice.[16]

It was nevertheless a terrible warning to the Ikkō-ikki, and the long and bitter war between them and Nobunaga was to last a full decade. Oda Nobunaga's last campaign against the Ishiyama Honganji finished in August 1580 after ten years of intermittent but bitter fighting that involved many features beyond siege work and assault. One crucial tactic was to deny the Ishiyama Honganji any support from fellow *monto* or sympathetic *daimyō*. By 1574 their comrades on the Nagashima delta near modern Nagoya had been eliminated. In 1575, the same year as his famous victory at the battle of Nagashino, Oda Nobunaga swept through Echizen province against its Ikkō-ikki forces in a savage campaign that put even the destruction of Enryakuji into the shade. Nobunaga was pleased with the results, which he described in letters that emphasized his contempt for the lower-class *monto*. Words like 'eradicate' and 'wipe out' flowed from his brush.[17] When he attacked Fuchu (now the town of Takefu) he wrote two letters from the site.[18] One contained the chilling statement, 'As for the town of Fuchu, only dead bodies can be seen without any empty space left between them. I would like to show it to you. Today I will search the mountains and the valleys and kill everybody.' By November 1575 he could boast that he had 'wiped out several tens of thousands of the villainous rabble in Echizen and Kaga'. In *Shinchōkōki*, Nobunaga's biographer reported that from the 15th to the 19th of the eighth lunar month of 1575, a total of 12,250 people were seized. Nobunaga gave orders to his pages to execute the prisoners, while his troops took countless men and women with them to their respective home provinces.[19]

Nobunaga also made clever use of the jealousy that still existed between the Honganji and the smaller rival branches of Jōdo Shinshū. Any Honganji *monto* who survived his attacks were given the opportunity to change their allegiance. For example, a surviving letter from Nobunaga to the Senpukuji in Mino province in 1572 gives the temple two days to renounce its affiliation to Osaka. Additionally, a prolonged naval campaign was designed to cut Mōri's supply lines until, isolated from any support, Ishiyama Honganji surrendered.

The death of Baba Nobuharu, one of the Takeda 'Twenty-Four Generals', at the battle of Nagashino in 1575, the great victory secured by Oda Nobunaga.

One curious feature of the Honganji's collapse was that its final surrender occurred after peace negotiations conducted by the imperial court. Emperor Ogimachi proposed peace on the instigation of Nobunaga, who was quite clearly the driving force behind the negotiations. Why Nobunaga chose to approach the Honganji through the imperial court is something of a mystery, but it shows the respect in which the imperial institution was still held. Oaths were signed in blood by both sides, and the inhabitants of Ishiyama Honganji thronged out of the fortress unharmed, scurrying off 'like baby spiders'.[20] That night the entire complex burst into flames and was utterly destroyed, probably on the initiative of the Ikkō-ikki leaders themselves, who did not wish their glorious headquarters to become a prize for the man they had defied for so long.

Nobunaga's war against the Ikkō-ikki is commonly regarded as having finished with the surrender of Ishiyama Honganji in 1580. However, bitter fighting continued for a few years. The first action was directed against Kaga province, where die-hard elements among the Ikkō-ikki abandoned the flat plains and entrenched themselves in fortified temples in the surrounding mountainous areas. The sites were to change hands three times within the following two years. In 1582 the temple castles were taken by Nobunaga and destroyed; this time no chance of resurgence was to be allowed. First, 300 men of the Ikkō-ikki were crucified on the river bed, and after this gruesome display the inhabitants of the local villages were annihilated.[21]

FROM WARRIORS TO WORSHIPPERS

Oda Nobunaga died in 1582, and three years later his successor, Toyotomi Hideyoshi, finally quelled militant Buddhism. The last Jōdo Shinshū enclaves – known as the Saiga Ikkō-ikki – were located in Kii province to the south of Osaka, around the area where the castle and city of Wakayama now stand. Not far away was the other remaining religious army in Japan: the *sōhei* of Negorodera, who had very unwisely fought against Hideyoshi during the Komaki campaign of 1584. This folly brought terrible retribution upon them the following year. The result was the near-total destruction of the Negorodera complex in as thorough a job as Nobunaga had performed on Hieizan. Hideyoshi then turned his attentions towards the Saiga Ikkō-ikki, and the last armed enclave of Jōdo Shinshū disappeared from Japan.

To underline his triumph, in 1585 Hideyoshi sent the following warning to the Shingon temples on Kōyasan that same year:

Item: The monks, priests in the world and others have not been prudent in their religious studies. The manufacture and retention of senseless weapons, muskets and the like is treacherous and wicked.

The *monto* of the Ikkō-ikki prepare to defend their temple. From a hanging scroll in the Rennyo Kinenkan, Yoshizaki.

Item: In as much as you saw with your own eyes that Hieizan and Negorodera were finally destroyed for acting with enmity against the realm, you should be discerning in this matter.[22]

The authorities on Mount Kōya were not slow to grasp the point. In 1588, when Toyotomi Hideyoshi enacted his famous 'Sword Hunt' to disarm the peasantry, the monks of Kōyasan were the first to respond by handing over their cache of

This statue of Amida Buddha rightfully has pride of place in the modern Yoshizakiji at Yoshizaki.

A hanging scroll depicting
Amida Buddha in the
museum of Yoshizakiji
in Yoshizaki.

arms. Meanwhile Kennyo sought every opportunity to restore the cathedral of
Jōdo Shinshū, but only as a religious headquarters, not as a fortress. The
opportunity came after Kennyo sent some of the few remaining Ikkō-ikki
warriors to help Hideyoshi during the Shizugatake campaign in 1583. In
gratitude to the *monto*, Hideyoshi eventually made a parcel of land available in
Kyōto in 1589, and the Honganji headquarters were rebuilt there in 1591.

Hideyoshi's successor, Tokugawa Ieyasu (1542–1616), was never a man to
take chances. Considering very seriously any possibility of an Ikkō-ikki revival,
he gave high priority to the issue, resolving it in 1602, the year before he was
officially proclaimed Shogun. The results may be seen by any visitor to Kyōto
today, where there are two Jōdo Shinshū temples called Nishi (Western)

Honganji and Higashi (Eastern) Honganji, both of which appear to be the headquarters of the same organization. A dispute between Junnyo, who headed the Honganji, and his older brother Gyonyo provided Ieyasu with the pretext he needed for dividing the sect. Ieyasu backed Gyonyo and founded Higashi Honganji to rival the existing one, henceforth called Nishi Honganji, built by Hideyoshi in 1591. This weakened the political power of the sect, leaving it as a strong religious organization, but never again capable of transforming itself into a monk army.

Jōdo Shinshū is today the largest Buddhist organization in Japan, a worthy acknowledgement of the genuinely populist roots that Shinran and Rennyo laid down so many centuries ago. Toyotomi Hideyoshi had already paid a compliment to the Ikkō-ikki in 1586, admiring the *monto* for their fine strategic eye. To hold out for ten years against Oda Nobunaga proved that the site of Ishiyama Honganji was a superb strategic and defensive location. Recalling how it had frustrated his master for so long, he chose it as the site for Osaka castle, Japan's largest fortress. In 1615 it required Japan's most massive siege using European artillery to crush it, and nowadays it lies at the centre of Japan's second city – the great modern metropolis of Osaka.

ONWARD, CHRISTIAN SAMURAI!

As mentioned throughout this book, not only do Japan's various religious traditions intermingle, but the Japanese have always seemed content to take part in different religious rites. At the time of the samurai, foreign and indigenous elements were blended institutionally and ritually in a coherent whole that was largely cooperative. The anger of Nichiren was directed at those whom he reckoned had sullied the purity of the faith that otherwise they all so firmly maintained.

In the mid-16th century, however, a new religion arrived – Christianity. The European import of Christianity was to show an intolerance that went far beyond the wrath of Nichiren. When confrontation occurred between Christianity and the religions that were already established in Japan, the Christian attitude was one of no compromise. Rather than formulating their own version of the *honji suijaku* theory – which might have suggested that Christ, wishing to save all deluded sentient beings, had manifested himself as the *kami* – the native gods of Japan were simply denounced as devils. Their shrines were destroyed and their statues burned by fervent converts. When the reaction against Christianity began, an equivalent intolerance was pursued against this exclusivist and intrusive foreign creed, with tragic consequences for its adherents.

Just as Buddhism had been carried to Japan on the waves of the elegant culture of Tang China, so was Christianity conveyed to Japan on the choppier seas of 16th-century European learning and technology. The arrival of Christianity in Japan in 1549 had been preceded only six years earlier by the unexpected landfall of the first Europeans. On 23 September 1543 a group of

OPPOSITE

The classic image of the death-defying samurai swordsman, to whom the world of the sacred was an ever-present reality. A Christian samurai was no different from any other in his attitude to fighting.

excited Japanese peasants on the island of Tanegashima discovered, anchored in a cove, a Chinese junk driven there by storms. On board the ship were two Portuguese merchants.[1] As Japan's first European visitors the men were interesting enough, but what particularly excited the owner of the island were the matchlock muskets that they possessed. These weapons were the first firearms to be seen in Japan.[2] The local *daimyō* Tanegashima Tokitaka (1528–79) had to have them, and, according to the traditional account of the subsequent negotiations, money changed hands. European trade with Japan had begun.

Soon the traders were joined by priests, the link between merchant and missionary proving invaluable in the propagation of the gospel. Over the following half century, Portuguese and Spanish traders and missionaries dominated relationships between Europe and Japan. Spain and Portugal became a joint monarchy in 1580, a political factor that enhanced their monopoly of Japanese trade until 1600, when the arrival of the English and Dutch began a long association between Protestant Europe and Japan that eventually eclipsed the Spanish and Portuguese efforts.[3] After 1639, when Catholic nations were expelled as a result of the *Sakoku* (Closed Country) policy, Dutch trading activities continued, but were confined to the artificial island of Dejima in Nagasaki harbour. As English interests had ended in 1623, this became the sole gateway for contact until the opening-up of Japan in the 19th century.

The Christian mission to Japan has a definite starting point of the Feast of the Assumption, 15 August 1549, when St Francis Xavier stepped ashore at Kagoshima.[4] Thus began a period of missionary activity lasting about 90 years, which is conventionally and conveniently labelled the 'Christian Century', although for the majority of Japanese, Christianity remained a marginal influence during this time. Nevertheless, Xavier's well-known comments from 5 November 1549 that the Japanese were 'the best who have yet been discovered' were echoed by his successor Valignano, who believed that Japan was the most important missionary ground in the East.[5]

The Jesuit pioneer was to find, as the merchants had already realized, that he had arrived in Japan at a time of political turmoil. Both religious and commercial enterprises needed safe harbours – literally and metaphorically – where their endeavours might flourish. The skill lay in finding a leader who not only had influence and sympathy but enough political acumen to ensure that his head remained securely on his shoulders. Initially, a handful of Japan's warring *daimyō* appeared to fall into this very exclusive category. All were located in Kyūshū, Japan's southernmost main island where Xavier had landed, and their hospitality to the missionaries went some way towards alleviating the dreadful start that Christian evangelization suffered. To put it mildly, something of the Christian message became lost in translation. Xavier's first guide to Japan, a reformed pirate called Yajirō, seemed to have understood the religious beliefs of his native land as poorly as the Christianity that he had absorbed in an eight-month-long crash course. As a result Xavier found himself preaching to Japanese whom he had been wrongly informed worshipped one God, about a Christian deity whom he unintentionally equated with Mahāvairocana Buddha through his use of the Japanese title of Dainichi.[6]

If Yajirō's clumsy stab at comparative religion had any positive outcome then it was that the confusion (and in one instance the 'jeers and laughter')[7] that the message caused bought time for the Jesuits to establish themselves. That, combined with the desires of sympathetic *daimyō* to attract Portuguese ships to their own harbours, gave Christianity a secure if somewhat baffling start in Japan. Determined to take his message to the top, Xavier proceeded to Kyōto, but he was unable to gain an audience either with the Shogun or the emperor. He came to two conclusions: first, that some of the *daimyō* were more important than Japan's supposed rulers, and second that if he wanted to influence anyone then he had to 'lift his act'. So in 1551 Xavier made his second visit to Ouchi Yoshitaka (1507–51), a *daimyō* whom he had identified as a key figure. His first visit to Ouchi's capital of Yamaguchi, when Xavier had behaved almost as a supplicant, had been a failure. The second attempt, when he turned up dressed as an ambassador and bearing gifts and credentials, had a very positive effect. The Jesuits were allotted a vacant Buddhist monastery and allowed both to preach and to convert. It was the beginning of a policy of relying on the *daimyō* that was to be the hallmark of Christian success. But which *daimyō* could be relied upon? Alas, not Yoshitaka, because he was overthrown in 1551 and 'avenged' by the decidedly unsympathetic Mōri Motonari at the battle of Miyajima in 1555. As a result, in 1557 the Jesuit church in Yamaguchi became a Buddhist temple once again.

The mission fared better with Otomo Sōrin (1530–87) in Bungo province. Sōrin was helpful from the time he first met Xavier in 1551, even accepting baptism in 1578. This made him the most celebrated of the *Kirishitan daimyō*, although he was not the first to earn the prefix. In 1559 Father Gaspar Vilela, helped enormously by a letter of introduction from Sōrin, gained Shogunal permission to preach in the area of Kyōto. Here he came up against the suspicions of Matsunaga Hisahide (1510–77), a fervent adherent of the Nichiren sect, whose initial sympathies with the Christian preachers were reversed when complaints were received from

Otomo Sōrin, the *daimyō* of Bungo province. Sōrin was helpful from the time he first met St Francis Xavier in 1551, and even accepted baptism himself in 1578.

OPPOSITE

Matsunaga Hisahide was a master of the tea ceremony, and when he was forced to commit suicide after his castle fell he began by smashing his favourite priceless tea kettle so that it would not fall into the hands of his enemies.

Buddhist priests in the capital that the missionaries were undermining Japanese tradition. Hisahide generously instituted an enquiry into the disruptive religion under three prominent scholars. The process had a very unexpected outcome, because by the end of the sitting all three had converted to Christianity – and without a single juicy Portuguese ship in sight!

Matsunaga Hisahide, who cannot have been pleased at the outcome, is an interesting character in the history of the samurai and the sacred whose life reflects several of the themes explored in this book. As a statesman he was a 'kingmaker' of Shoguns. As a samurai warrior he made an important contribution to Japanese military architecture with the erection of Tamon castle. Father Almeida visited it in April 1565,[8] and it is partly from his description that the conclusion has been drawn that Tamon possessed Japan's first tower keep, although no trace of it now remains.[9] As a member of the Nichiren sect of Buddhism, Hisahide displayed that organization's characteristic intolerance of other sects, to the extent that he is usually blamed for one of the major acts of religious vandalism in Japanese history: the destruction by fire, for the second time, of Emperor Shōmu's glorious Tōdaiji in Nara. The temple, including the rebuilt hall housing the re-cast Great Buddha, went up in smoke in 1567.[10] Luis Frois, however, tells a different story:

> A large part of the army which besieged the fortress of Tamonyama was encamped in this temple of the Daibut [*sic*] and throughout the precincts of this monastery. Among them was also a brave soldier – one who is well known to our people – who in his zeal for the religion and the worship appropriate solely to the Creator of the Universe, without being persuaded to do so by any man, while on guard duty at night secretly set fire to the place. And so everything that was there burned down, with nothing left standing except a gate which was situated far away at the entrance.[11]

Taira Shigehira had burned Nara in 1181 as an act of war. An anonymous Christian samurai seems to have repeated the act in 1567 as an act of faith. But Matsunaga Hisahide, exonerated by Frois' revelation, had enough blood on his hands from his deposing of the Shogun Ashikaga Yoshiteru. Eventually forced to commit suicide in 1577, he nevertheless made a dramatic contribution to the mythology of the samurai and the sacred. Hisahide had always sought spiritual solace in the quasi-religious ritual of the tea ceremony with its strong links to Zen Buddhism (see pp. 140–145). Before committing the act of *seppuku* – the painful version of suicide that involved cutting open one's abdomen – Hisahide took his most precious tea kettle and smashed it into a thousand pieces so that no other connoisseur would ever own it. To complete the theatre of death, his son dived head first from the parapet of Shikizan castle with his sword halfway down his throat.[12]

Back in Kyūshū, the Christian faith was being spread by men who were willing to perform acts of cultural mayhem every bit as ruthless as the burning of Nara. To the Jesuits, however, leaders like Otomo Sōrin looked increasingly like an answer to prayer. In 1578, in return for help with his marital problems, Sōrin accepted baptism, proclaiming that his subjects 'would all have to become Christians and live with each other in brotherly love and concord'.[13] To help the brotherly love on its way Sōrin instituted a policy of persecution of Buddhist and Shintō priests and the destruction of their property. He was currently expanding his territories into Hyūga province, where such havoc was pursued even more intensely than in Bungo. Though an eye-witness account of these activities does not exist, they probably differed little from the actions of Antonio Koteda of Ikitsuki who 'had no greater pleasure in the world than to see them pull down idols out of the temples and houses, and burn them and throw them in to the sea'.[14] Luis Frois wrote the following account of another prominent Christian convert, Omura Sumitada (baptized as Bartolemeo):

> As Dom Bartholomeo had gone off to the wars, it so happened that he passed on the way an idol, Marishiten by name, which is their god of battles. When they pass it, they bow and pay reverence to it, and the pagans who are on horseback dismount as a sign of their respect. Now the idol had above it a cockerel. As the *tono* [lord] came there with his squadron he had his men stop and ordered them to take the idol and burn it together with the whole temple; and he took the cockerel and gave it a blow with the sword, saying to it, 'Oh, how many times have you betrayed me!' And after everything had been burnt down, he had a very beautiful cross erected on the same spot, and after he and his men had paid very deep reverence to it, they continued on their way to the wars.[15]

Sōrin's approach to the coexistence of his native gods beside the Christian import was similarly straightforward, and it is instructive to compare this attitude with that of non-Christian samurai generals to whom temple-burning was also not entirely unknown. A certain Hosokawa Akiuji burned several temples and shrines to the ground during one battle, then was so stricken with remorse that he shaved his head and became a monk.[16] Sōrin's temple-burning was deliberate and remorseless, ending in disaster. To the south of the newly acquired Otomo land of Hyūga lay the territories of the mighty Shimazu family. St Francis Xavier had first landed in the Shimazu home province of Satsuma, but finding his hosts lukewarm he had moved on. In 1578, as part of their 'manifest destiny' to conquer the whole of Kyūshū, the Shimazu samurai invaded Hyūga. To those of the Otomo army who were not well versed in Japanese heraldry, the approach of a huge army carrying banners that bore a symbol of a cross (usually displayed within a circle and probably derived from the design of a horse's bit) might have been encouraging. But there was no

When the persecution of Christians began some brave believers held secret prayer meetings in their homes. This is a waxworks display in Oe depicting some secret Christians worshipping in a store room.

Christian connection in their appearance, and no sympathy in their intentions. Just before they clashed in battle the war gods granted their leader Shimazu Yoshihisa a dream, as a result of which he composed a poem: 'The enemy's defeated host/Is as the maple leaves of autumn,/Floating on the water/Of the Takuta stream.'[17] Yoshihisa's dream proved to be a good omen for the Shimazu. Nearby were two large ponds, where many of the Christian Otomo samurai who fell in the subsequent battle of Mimigawa died; the flags floating in the water looked like maple leaves. Even Otomo Sōrin's prized pair of bronze cannon, a present from the Portuguese that represented the state of the art in military technology, fell as prizes to the victors. The Shimazu's victory meant the end of the Otomo as a force in Kyūshū. Fabian Fucan, the author of a polemic against Christianity, was later to use Mimigawa as an example of what happened to a *daimyō* when he forsakes the worship of the gods and Buddhas for a foreign religion:

> Look! Look at Otomo Sōrin of Bungo. In the days when Sōrin was still devoted to the Buddhas and *kami* he brandished his power over all of Kyūshū and the glory of his name spread throughout the four seas. But after he entered the ranks of *Deus* the fortunes of war suddenly turned against him. With his eldest son Yoshimune he fell over Hyūga to fight the Shimazu, suffered a crushing defeat at Mimigawa, and had to flee home deserted by all and in desperate straits. After that his house gradually fell to ruin, so prosperous, so flourishing for many generations, the family is practically extinct today. And are any offspring left, or not? Such is the sad state of the house at present.[18]

Pragmatic to the end, the Jesuits drowned their sorrows over Sōrin's demise two years later when they received the gift of an important piece of Japanese real estate: the harbour of Nagasaki. It was presented to the Order in 1580 by Omura Bartolemeo Sumitada, who had made his entire province Christian. His gift infuriated the neighbouring *daimyō*, Matsuura Takanobu (the father of Shigenobu, with whom this book began), not because of any apparent capitulation to the Christians, but because Takanobu had wanted them to make his port of Hirado into their base. Fortified by the Jesuits, Nagasaki was to remain a centre of European influence on Japan long after the Christian missionaries had gone. The sole Dutch trading post after the expulsion was to be set up on Dejima.

Any fears of a possible expulsion were far from the minds of the missionaries in 1580. This was, after all, the year when Oda Nobunaga, who regarded religion as a means of social control, had finally overcome the 'Devil's Christianity' practised by the *monto* of Jōdo Shinshū. The rise of Oda Nobunaga, whose power was to eclipse that of all his contemporaries, proved a blessing to the Jesuits. In as much as he was interested in any religious ideas – or even ideals – at all, he was sympathetic to Christianity. The economic and military power of the Ikkō-ikki and their sympathizers, many of whom

The harbour of Nagasaki was donated to the Jesuits by Omura Sumitada and became an important centre of Christianity and European contact. It was fortified but had to be handed over to Toyotomi Hideyoshi after his invasion of Kyūshū in 1587.

supported them simply because they opposed Nobunaga, gave him a listening ear for these strange foreigners who had access to modern military technology and preached a message that was furiously anti-Buddhist. The fact that their gospel was one of opposition to Japanese religion *per se*, while Nobunaga was opposed merely to the use of it against him, was overlooked by the Jesuits in their delight at the freedom they enjoyed.

LORDS AND LOYALTIES

Nobunaga's careless encouragement was an arrangement that suited both sides, but what did it really mean to be a Christian samurai? Christ's teaching about turning the other cheek is conspicuous by its absence from a society where the notion of the vendetta was a solemn duty,[19] while any suggestion that 'Thou shalt not kill' was ignored as thoroughly in Japan as it was in contemporary Europe. The Jesuits, after all, had come to Japan from a continent torn by religious warfare, where the Church's advice never seemed to be one of surrender. In 1511 Europe had even witnessed the unique sight of an armoured pope when, confident that he was fighting a just war for the sake of his faith, Pope Julius II fought his anti-French campaign. The leaders of Europe were advised as early as 1502 by a certain Robert de Balsac that when a prince went to war, his first consideration should be that his cause was just; the second consideration was whether or not he had enough artillery.[20]

One pay-off for having Christian samurai in your armies was suggested by the Jesuits, who argued strongly that Christian converts would show greater loyalty to their *daimyō* because betrayal was contrary to the Christian faith. This was quite a claim to make by men who recognized a higher authority than any that could be possessed by a temporal prince. Betrayal may have been contrary to Christian teaching, but with whom did a Christian samurai's ultimate loyalty lie? Put another way, what were the limits of loyalty? The persecutions that Christians were to suffer under Hideyoshi and Ieyasu arose partly from the answer that these two statesmen provided to that question. They concluded that the demands of Christianity could, under certain circumstances, require a believer to revolt against his rightful ruler, an action that could not be tolerated.

Back in 1577, the Jesuits' claims appeared to be confirmed by comments made to Nobunaga by his follower Araki Murashige. Though Murashige could not explain the teachings of the missionaries whom he allowed in his domain, he did know that all his Christian vassals were remarkably obedient to him. Yet it was this same Araki Murashige whose actions were to put that statement to the ultimate test. In 1578 he deserted Nobunaga and joined the coalition forces against him, taking his loyal Christian retainers with him. Among them was Takayama Ukon (1553–1615), who had received the baptismal name of Justo.

Ukon pursued throughout his domains the now familiar pattern of forced conversions and destruction of non-Christian artefacts and buildings. He was destined to combine to a greater degree than any of his contemporaries the discordant roles of bloodthirsty samurai commander and saintly Christian warrior. Throughout his long career Ukon remained the darling of the Jesuits. To a large extent their approval was justified, as he was one of the few senior members of the samurai class who remained staunch in the faith when times got rough. Most responded to persecution with apostasy. Ukon suffered exile to Manila, where he died in 1615.

In 1578 Ukon and his father held the castle of Takatsuki, which lay midway between Araki Murashige's headquarters and that of Nobunaga. Determined to have Takatsuki, Nobunaga callously manipulated Ukon's loyalty to his *daimyō*, to his faith and to the two family members he had been required to hand over to Araki Murashige as a guarantee of good behaviour. Using Father Organtino as his messenger and diplomat, Nobunaga threatened Ukon that if he did not hand over the castle to him then the Jesuit priests and their followers would all be crucified. If he joined Nobunaga, they would receive a free hand for proselytizing. In that case the hostages would of course die. Nobunaga's ultimatum exposes better than any other the cynical reasoning that lay behind his support for the missions. To complicate matters further, Ukon's father

Unzen, on the Shimabara peninsula, became the open-air torture chamber of the Nagasaki area. Nowadays Unzen is a popular hot-spring resort. This is one of the few large pools of boiling water to retain its appearance from the 17th century.

steadfastly refused to place their castle into Nobunaga's hands, an act that conflicted with Confucian ideals of filial piety.

Takayama Ukon decided that his loyalty lay at a higher level than to the turncoat Araki Murashige. It actually lay at two higher levels: that of Nobunaga and then God, in that order. By that decision Ukon betrayed the hostages and his own father. Takayama the elder went to Araki to explain how he had been thwarted by the machinations of his own son. Fortunately, that was enough to save the hostages, and they survived the affair unharmed. Nobunaga got his castle, the Christian mission survived and Ukon could salve his Christian conscience with the assurance that betraying a traitor provided a rare example of two wrongs making a right.[21]

Takayama Ukon was one of the most renowned *Kirishitan daimyō*. He served Nobunaga and Hideyoshi while still maintaining his faith, and was eventually exiled to Manila, where he died in 1615.

Clearly, extra loyalty was not necessarily part of the package of being a *Kirishitan*; however, there was a likelier pay-off in that samurai who embraced Christianity would probably demonstrate extra fighting spirit when set against enemies who still espoused the faith that they had been taught to denounce. That was to come true within a few years for the same Takayama Ukon. In 1582 Oda Nobunaga was overthrown and forced to commit suicide. Ukon fought loyally in the battle of Yamazaki that destroyed the usurper, but then fell foul of Toyotomi Hideyoshi, Nobunaga's successor, when on religious grounds he refused to offer incense on the Buddhist altar at Nobunaga's funeral. He redeemed himself by his participation in the battle of Shizugatake in 1583, and by enthusiastically taking part in Hideyoshi's destruction of the last of the Jōdo Shinshū supporters at Negorodera in 1585, a battle in which his anti-Buddhist convictions would have given him an easy conscience.

HIDEYOSHI AND THE CHRISTIANS

Toyotomi Hideyoshi began his reign in a manner that gave great encouragement to the missionaries. On one occasion he informed them that he might even consider becoming a Christian himself if the Church was willing to drop its ban on polygamy, but he was hardly earnest in his spiritual quest. Elison notes wryly that the interview took place on the appropriate date of April the First.[22] The reunification of Japan that Hideyoshi achieved was a far more serious matter than changing one religion for another. Lasting nine years between 1582 and 1591, the process included one operation in particular that was to have an important bearing on the future direction of Christianity in Japan: his conquest of Kyūshū in 1587. At the time when Hideyoshi intervened, the Shimazu of Satsuma had all but completed their conquest of the island. A request for help from Otomo Sōrin provided the pretext for Hideyoshi to mount the largest military operation seen in Japan up to that time. Among the *Kirishitan daimyō* who marched in Hideyoshi's armies was Takayama Ukon, whom the Jesuit accounts describe as setting off to war with a rosary round his neck. Some samurai bore the device of the cross on their flags; others had it lacquered on to the breastplates of their armour.[23] The Shimazu were overcome. While they and certain other *daimyō* were generously allowed to retain their territories, they found themselves with new neighbours whose reward for loyalty to Hideyoshi was increased land holdings in return for preventing a Shimazu resurgence.

At the conclusion of the Kyūshū campaign, one tiny corner of the island remained that belonged neither to a *daimyō* nor even to Hideyoshi: the Jesuit enclave of Nagasaki. From here, Father Gaspar Coelho travelled to meet

Hideyoshi in the Jesuits' private warship, which was reputed to be the fastest vessel in Japanese waters. The meeting was courteous, giving no indication of the shock that was to come only a few days later when Hideyoshi issued an edict condemning Christianity and giving the Jesuits 20 days to leave Japan. The document began with a statement that was to become depressingly familiar over the next few decades: 'Japan is the land of the gods.' Indeed it was, and the Christians had destroyed the shrines of the *kami* and the temples of the Buddhas, so they must be punished. The Jesuits were stunned, but Hideyoshi was determined to exercise control over the whole of Japan, just as he had done in Kyūshū.

The notice to quit Japan did not include merchants. This was made quite clear, as were several other points set out in a separate document issued the day before the edict, which provided important information about why the process of conquest had to contain measures to suppress Christianity. The Christian *daimyō* had instituted compulsory conversion for their subjects, a practice that could not be allowed to continue. By contrast, Buddhism had proved accommodative to the *kami* of Japan, just as it had absorbed the gods of India. The troublesome Jōdo Shinshū may have been a mass movement, but even it lay within a long tradition. Once shorn of its military strength it was capable of being controlled and turned into a positive force. Hideyoshi's restoration of the Honganji in Kyōto, an event that happened at about the same time that Christianity was feeling the force of a diametrically opposing attitude, went some way to restoring the medieval balance of power in all its mutually supportive glory. Christianity would accept no such compromise. Grave consequences awaited any expanding religion that went in for such practices as the wholesale destruction of shrines and temples. The Ikkō-ikki had needed war to bring them to their senses, so Hideyoshi drew a fateful parallel between his predecessor's need to destroy the Honganji and his present concerns with the Christian menace.

This direct comparison between the Ikkō-ikki and the Christians was eventually to prove to be the mission's death warrant.[24] The overthrow of the Togashi *daimyō* in Kaga and his replacement by a 'peasant government' of the Ikkō-ikki was compared to the antics of Christian *daimyō* such as Takayama Ukon. Could there have been a Christian coup in Japan? The concentration of many like-minded individuals in northern Kyūshū around the 'Jesuit colony' of Nagasaki indicated the possibility of an 'independent Christian Kyūshū' had the Shimazu not been around, but a more likely scenario was of the Christian *daimyō* supporting a foreign invasion. The size of Portuguese ships and the armaments they carried was well known to the Japanese. European military intervention in Japan may have been a remote possibility, but it is worth remembering that when Khubilai Khan invaded Japan in 1281, the *kami* had sent a tempest to destroy the invaders. In 1587 Hideyoshi had decided to launch a pre-emptive strike of his own against anyone who might aid such an invasion, and had blown his first blast as a warning.

Even if Christianity's 'militant wing' could be neutralized, why was the faith itself so unwelcome to Hideyoshi, when centuries before the introduction of Buddhism to the 'land of the gods' had proved so beneficial to the ruling elite? Buddhism's success is partly explained by the fact that it came to Japan gift-wrapped in the culture of Tang China. It provided a metaphysical underpinning for the assumption of power by the Yamato court, and the establishment of the system of government that came with it provided the stability that the rulers of Japan welcomed. Christianity offered nothing like this to Hideyoshi. The first guns had been welcome, but Japan now had its own ordnance production facilities. Rather than promising wealth and culture, Christianity presented the dreadful spectre of a re-run of Nobunaga's ten-year-long war against the Honganji.

When suspect Christians were interrogated, one test used was to require them to trample on an image of Christ to show their contempt for the faith. This surviving example of a *fumi-e* from Ikitsuki is a bronze plaque set in a wooden board. It has been worn away by many feet.

105

When the edict was issued there was some token persecution. As an example to the other Christian *daimyō*, Takayama Ukon was dispossessed and Nagasaki was confiscated. Some churches were destroyed and the missionary priests, fearing the consequences, kept their heads down. As far as the year 1587 was concerned, however, that was the extent of anti-Christian activity. Hideyoshi moved on to other concerns, even creating a renewed optimism among the shocked Jesuits when he began a bizarre fashion for wearing things European. The sight of Hideyoshi and his henchmen taking the air with rosaries and crucifixes round their necks produced a mixture of elation and confusion.

That Hideyoshi was probably wrong in his fears that Christians were a Fifth Column, and that the Jesuits were right in their claims that Christianity meant more loyalty to the temporal power rather than less, seemed to be illustrated in 1589 and again in 1590. Among the redistribution of fiefs in Kyūshū following the 1587 success, half of Higo province had gone to the staunch Christian Konishi Yukinaga. Twice he faced rebellion from within his new territory, and twice he put it down with great severity, even though three out of the five leaders of the *ikki* on the Amakusa islands were Christian. One wonders if the noble Takayama Ukon would have behaved any differently if his position had been threatened from within his own ranks. The likelihood that men like Konishi or Takayama could unite against Hideyoshi in the name of Christ seemed very remote indeed.

THE STRANGE CRUSADE

During the ten years that followed the 1587 edict the problems of the Christian *daimyō* faded beside the great enterprise of reuniting Japan under the sword of Hideyoshi. In 1588 he enacted his famous 'Sword Hunt', by which all weapons were to be confiscated from the peasantry and placed in the hands of loyal *daimyō* and their increasingly professional armies. By this act, the means of making war were forcibly removed from anyone of whom Hideyoshi did not approve, as the Sword Hunt was much more than a search of farmers' premises. Minor *daimyō* whose loyalty was suspect, religious institutions who had the capacity for armed rebellion and recalcitrant village headmen were all purged in an operation that parallels Henry VIII's Dissolution of the Monasteries. The victims were told that the swords, spears and guns would not be wasted, but would be melted down to make nails for the enormous image of the Buddha that Hideyoshi was erecting in Kyōto. The nation would therefore benefit from the operation in two ways. It would be spiritually blessed and would be freed from the curses of war and rebellion that had caused such disruption and suffering in the past.

Very few of the weapons ended up as nails. Most would have been stockpiled or reissued to Hideyoshi's armies when they overcame the remaining opponents to Hideyoshi's rule. By 1591 the reunification process was complete. Hideyoshi issued a further edict by which a strict separation was made between the military and agricultural functions. The Separation Edict defined the distinction between samurai and farmer that was to continue throughout the Tokugawa Period. No longer could a peasant – as Hideyoshi himself had once been – enlist as a foot soldier and rise to be a general. From now on a peasant who was forced (or even volunteered) to do his duty would not carry a sword or gun, but a cripplingly heavy pack on his back. To the leader of a modern army such as Hideyoshi such a restriction on military manpower was a matter of no concern. He had troops in easy sufficiency, and, because of the increased sophistication associated with modern weapons, an untrained and undrilled peasant handed an arquebus or a long-shafted spear would be a liability rather than an asset.

This rigid separation between soldiers and labourers was to become a noticeable feature of Hideyoshi's final military venture: the Korean campaign. His grand plan to conquer China, for which the subjugation of Korea was a geographical necessity if nothing else, was the natural progress of his achievement of complete power in Japan.[25] One other feature of Hideyoshi's Korean operation, which began with a seaborne invasion in 1592, was the presence in his army of a large number of Christian *daimyō*. This was largely because many had their fiefs in Kyūshū, and logistics meant that the nearer a *daimyō* was to the invasion headquarters of Hizen-Nagoya castle, the greater would be his obligation to supply men for the army. The First Division of the invading army included the *Kirishitan* contingents of Konishi Yukinaga, Sō Yoshitomo, Omura Yoshiaki and Arima Harunobu. So many crosses were flown from their banners that the whole enterprise, as Elison notes, gave the undertaking 'the air of a bizarre crusade'.[26]

The Christian samurai behaved with the loyalty that the Jesuits had once described to Nobunaga. Konishi Yukinaga led the initial assaults on the Korean coastal defences in and around Busan, becoming the first general to enter Seoul after a whirlwind advance. An interesting religious perspective on the operation is provided by the fact that in command of the Second Division was Katō Kiyomasa, an adherent of the Nichiren sect who rode into battle with '*Namu Myōhō Renge-kyō!*' emblazoned on his battle flag instead of a Christian cross. He and Konishi Yukinaga did not enjoy a good relationship.

Konishi Yukinaga, the Christian *daimyō* who led Hideyoshi's invasion of Korea. From his statue in Uto.

The Korean war also provides the only example in samurai history of the provision of a Christian chaplaincy to a Japanese army. This occurred during the occupation of Korea between the departure of the Japanese forces in 1593 and their return for a second invasion in 1597. The Spanish Jesuit Father Gregorio de Cespedes went to Korea in the winter of 1594/95 in the capacity of visiting chaplain to the Christians among the Japanese troops.[27] At the end of 1594 he visited Konishi Yukinaga's *wajō* (Japanese-style fortress) at Ungcheon, where, 'The Father and his companion had much to do, as all these Christians had neither heard mass nor sermon nor confessed themselves since they had left Japan for Korea.'[28] In his second letter home Father Gregorio notes that Ungcheon, in common with the other castles that provided the means of control, was built 'on a very high and craggy slope. When I have to go down for some confessions at night, it gives me much work, and when I go back I ride a horse and rest many times on the way.'[29] The Korean winter was an enormous trial to him:

> The cold in Korea is very severe and without comparison with that of Japan. All day long my limbs are half benumbed, and in the morning I can hardly move my hands to say Mass, but I keep myself in good health; thanks to God and the fruit that our lord is giving.[30]

Among the *Kirishitan daimyō* Kuroda Nagamasa is due for special praise. His men listened to two sermons a day, and Nagamasa himself practised his faith devoutly:

> in order to meditate on them at his leisure, he withdrew each day at certain hours, which were set aside for this purpose, to read his books of devotion... Being such a great lord and such a leading soldier and commander, and busy in affairs of war, never did he abstain from fasting all the days ordered by the Church, without counting others which he added on account of his devoutness, all of which he accompanied with the secret disciplines which he practised.[31]

As Father Gregorio was the first European visitor to Korea it is sad that the only Koreans he ever came into contact with were those unfortunates captured by the Japanese and destined to be sent to Japan into slavery. The account of his mission notes an act of charity on the part of at least one member of the occupying forces:

> There was a knight, a native of Bungo, who, being in the war in Korea, and taking pity on the many creatures who were dying destitute of their parents, took it upon himself to baptise them because, since he could no longer make their bodies whole, they should not lose their souls. Thus all those whom he saw in probable danger of death he immediately baptised. For this purpose he had a servant of his always carry a bottle of water hanging from his belt and by these means he sent to heaven more than 200 souls.[32]

Father Gregorio concludes his brief correspondence with some personal yet perceptive observations of the Korean scene:

> All these Christians are very poor, and suffer from hunger, cold, illness and other inconveniences very different from conditions in other places. Although Hideyoshi sends food, so little reaches here that it is impossible to sustain all with them, and moreover the help that comes from Japan is insufficient and comes late. It is now two months since ships have come, and many crafts were lost.[33]

The survivors of this military disaster were sent back to invade Korea for a second time in 1597, but not before that year had witnessed an ominous development in the history of Christianity in Japan. In 1593, while many Christian samurai were fighting and dying in Korea, the Jesuits, who had enjoyed a monopoly of evangelization since Xavier's day, were joined by a group of Franciscan friars sent from the Philippines. The Franciscans behaved with the characteristic populist ardour of their Order. Their behaviour contrasted with the attitude of the Jesuits, who had focused their efforts largely on the upper reaches of Japanese society. An additional element of friction lay in the Spanish sponsorship of the Franciscans and the Portuguese patronage of the Society of

The martyrdom by crucifixion of the Twenty-Six Saints of Japan in February 1597, from an oil painting in the Sotome Museum.

The monument in Nagasaki to the Twenty-Six Saints of Japan, martyred under Hideyoshi.

Jesus. But these internal differences need not have caused problems to the Japanese mission had it not been for a most unfortunate shipwreck. As events were to prove, much more than a ship went aground on the rocks of Japan.

In October 1596 the *San Felipe* was wrecked off the coast of Shikoku. Hideyoshi ordered that the cargo should be confiscated, and the ship's pilot, hoping to forestall the action, became very belligerent. He threatened Hideyoshi's officials, warning them of the power of his Spanish masters and the wealth and resources of the Spanish Empire. His loose tongue also spoke of the way that previous Spanish conquests had begun – by 'softening up' the target country using priests. The story got back to Hideyoshi, who began to suspect that the Spanish Franciscans were spies sent to prepare the way for the foreign invasion he had always feared. Knowing much about invading a foreign country, Hideyoshi was unwilling to listen to Franciscan protests that the Jesuits were trying to frame them.

Hideyoshi took action, and the 16th-century *kami kaze* finally blew with all its force to scatter a non-existent invasion fleet. No ships were smashed to matchwood in his blast. Instead the typhoon hit the Christian mission, and Japan witnessed its first acts of martyrdom by the crucifixion on 5 February 1597 of St Paul Miki and companions: the Twenty-Six Saints of Japan. Their company, which consisted of six Franciscan missionaries, three Jesuits and 17 Japanese laymen, died on a hill overlooking Nagasaki harbour. From this moment, the history of Christianity in Japan took a different turn. From being proud and confident the Christian enterprise slowly went into reverse. There were no more martyrdoms under Hideyoshi, who had not long to live. His disastrous second invasion of Korea was launched within months of the Nagasaki martyrdoms. As Hideyoshi descended into megalomania the samurai were gradually driven out of the Korean peninsula by the joint efforts of Korea and Ming China. Hideyoshi died while his troops were fighting their last rearguard actions, and the defeated samurai – Christian and Buddhist alike – came sadly home.

THE SAMURAI AND THE SECRET

Within two years of Hideyoshi's death, Christianity in Japan, already changed in spirit by the martyrdoms of Nagasaki, also changed somewhat in form by the replication in Japan of the profound division within Christendom that had scarred 16th-century Europe. The Jesuits, who already had problems explaining their faith to increasingly hostile rulers, now also had to explain why the Christianity that they had left behind in Europe was far from being a seamless robe. For the first time in Japan they had to face up to the fact that there was something called Protestantism.

Unlike the Catholic missionaries who followed the Portuguese merchants, the first Protestant visitors to Japan were not succeeded by Lutheran or Calvinist pastors. The sole concern of the Dutch and English was trade. Conversion of Japanese people was of no interest to them; the only religious element in their make-up was a strong antagonism to Catholicism. The Dutch had been fighting a war of independence from Catholic Spain for many years, and the first Englishman to visit Japan, the famous William Adams, had been the captain of a ship that fought the Spanish Armada.[1] Apart from this knee-jerk reaction, which their Japanese hosts picked up on very quickly, their attitude towards religious matters in general was one of non-interest, and towards Japanese religion – whatever that was – one of utter and complete ignorance shrouded in a cloak of 17th-century prejudice. On 30 January 1622 Richard Cocks of the East India Company wrote the following in his diary:

> And so we went to the Hollanders to dinner, and they came to us for supper, we having in the afternoon visited the pagoda of Ottongo Fachemon [Hachiman], the

god of war, which out of doubt is the devil, for the picture showeth it, made in form as they paint the devil, and mounted upon a wild boar without bridle or saddle, and hath wings on his shoulders, as Mercury is painted to have.[2]

In other words, this 'Hachiman' must be the devil because his picture matched the description Cocks had learned from his childhood. Though the revelation did not excite within Cocks' breast any desire to burn down the shrine, the Jesuits' own converts could not have provided a better example of naïve condemnation.

The first Dutch ship to visit Japan was the sole survivor of a fleet of five vessels that left Rotterdam on 27 June 1598. Arriving off Bungo province on 9 April 1600, the lucky ship was the *Liefde*, which became the first vessel of any nation to reach Japan from Europe via the Straits of Magellan.[3] To complete a trio of 'firsts', also on board the *Liefde* was William Adams (mentioned above), the first Englishman to set foot in Japan.[4] The threat that their arrival posed to the existing Iberian trading hegemony became immediately apparent when the Portuguese insisted to anyone who would listen that the 'land of the gods' had just taken delivery of 'a party of piratical heretics'. This unflattering complaint was made forcibly to Tokugawa Ieyasu, who is referred to by Adams as 'the great king of the land' – a prescient statement, for this was effectively what Ieyasu was shortly to become.[5] As well as apprehending the crew, Ieyasu confiscated the armament of the *Liefde*, some of which may have been used at his decisive victory at the battle of Sekigahara on 21 October 1600.[6]

Tokugawa Ieyasu was one of history's great survivors. Taken as a hostage when a child, and made to fight for one of Japan's least successful *daimyō* when

Tokugawa Ieyasu, the first Tokugawa Shogun, shown here in a shrine to him in Okazaki.

a young man, he gradually asserted his independence and allied himself in turn with Nobunaga and Hideyoshi. As an adherent of the Jōdo sect, much of his early military experience consisted of defending his domain against the Ikkō-ikki. He eventually settled in eastern Japan on land presented to him by a grateful Hideyoshi. Its distance from Kyūshū allowed him to avoid service in Korea, which ensured that his troops were in better shape than those of many of his rivals who had suffered in that conflict. The battle of Sekigahara made Ieyasu ruler of Japan, and three years later he revived the post and title of Shogun. He made his own castle town into Japan's administrative capital. Known as Edo, it proved to be a highly successful choice, as may be judged from the fact that Edo is now known as Tokyo.

The year that saw the initial triumph of the first Tokugawa Shogun also marked the beginning of a partnership between Japan and her new arrivals from the Netherlands. On the last day of the momentous year of 1600, Queen Elizabeth I put her signature on the Royal Charter that gave birth to the 'Company of Merchants of London trading into the East Indies' – commonly known as the East India Company (EIC).[7] English trade with Japan was first mooted in 1608, when John Saris, an official in the EIC's factory in Bantam in Java, submitted a report to the Company's directors in which he suggested that, in contrast to the tropical East Indies, colder Japan would provide a market for English woollen broadcloth.[8] Further impetus was provided by the news of the establishment of a Dutch factory (trading post) in Hirado in 1609,[9] where, according to William Adams in a letter of 23 October 1611, 'the Hollanders have here an Indies of money'.[10] Thus convinced, the EIC directors agreed that relations with Japan should be pursued.

The first EIC vessel to sail to Japan was the *Clove*. It reached Japan, with the enthusiastic John Saris on board, on 11 June 1613. The ship docked at Hirado where the Dutch were already established. The Dutch provided no opposition, and the Englishmen were warmly welcomed by the local *daimyō*, Matsuura Shigenobu, whose prayers to Hachiman before the Korean campaign had seen him return home safely and prosper since then. The party headed east to meet Tokugawa Ieyasu at Shizuoka. Ieyasu had by then retired from the post of Shogun, so this audience was followed by a visit to Ieyasu's son, the new Shogun Tokugawa Hidetada (1579–1632), in Edo. When John Saris sailed from Japan on 5 December 1613 he left behind a factory on Hirado staffed by five Englishmen. Richard Cocks was appointed as its director, while Saris spent many long months travelling between England and Japan. Writing to the EIC in October 1614, he suggested those items that might be most advantageously sold to Japan, including 'pictures, painted, some lascivious, others of stories of wars by sea and land, the larger the better'.[11]

Over the next two decades the diaries, reports and correspondence of the EIC painted a vivid picture of political developments in Japan and the relationship between the samurai and the traders' perception of the sacred. On 20 June 1618 Richard Cocks wrote about how he had come face to face with a rather unpleasant warrior, an account that shows he had a complete understanding of the samurai's position in society:

> A mad gentleman (it is said) having been possessed with the devil more than a year past, was at this day at a banquet with his father, brother, wife and kindred, they persuading him to be better advised and leave off such courses. But on a sudden, before it could be prevented, he started up and drew out a *cattan* [the katana – the Japanese samurai sword] and cut off his brothers head, wounded his father, almost cutting off his arm, and cut his wife behind her shoulder on her back, that her entrails appeared, wounded diverse others, and slew out right his steward (or chief man). And yet it is thought nothing will be said to him, they which he hath killed being his kindred and servants, he being a gentleman.[12]

Cocks' main dealings with the samurai class were mediated through the Matsuura family who ruled the territory where the English factory was located and had to be kept sweet. This did not always work out, as on 10 August 1617, when 'the king's brother sent back the parrot I gave him, to keep her, she being sick, or I rather think to have a better present sent in place, for the parrot is well'.[13] Cocks was always intrigued by Japanese religion, even if he did not understand it. In 1614 he went to see a newly built pagoda erected in memory of two men who had killed themselves to accompany the late emperor in death.[14] By comparison, Catholicism was something he both understood and despised, particularly in the means by which it was disseminated among the Japanese, as this diary entry suggests:

> November 30 1617. I received a letter from Mr. Wickham to report popish miracles, how a man's arm was dried up for offering to burn a friar's cope or vestment, his arm standing stiff out, he not being able to pull it back nor bend it. Thus do these Popish priests invent lies to deceive the poor simple people.[15]

As for politics, several letters describe how in 1614 Toyotomi Hideyori, the surviving son of Toyotomi Hideyoshi, rebelled against Tokugawa rule. Regarding Ieyasu as a usurper, Hideyori packed Osaka castle with thousands of *rōnin* (masterless samurai) who had been dispossessed since Sekigahara,[16] many of whom were Christians. English and Dutch cannon, which were monsters compared with the Japanese varieties, played a vital role in crushing them. For the next couple of years Dutch and English trade flourished, but a decline began following the death of Tokugawa Ieyasu in 1616. Hidetada was far less sympathetic towards European contacts than his father had been, and decreed that trade was to be confined to Hirado and Nagasaki. His decision may have been due to pressure from Japanese merchants, but it also involved the underlying fears of Christian subversion and foreign intervention which the Osaka operation had highlighted once again.

In spite of these fears Christian martyrdom and persecution during the first few years of the Tokugawa Shogunate were sporadic throughout Japan, and were interspersed by periods of calm during which the Church more than held its own. The major shift in policy came with Ieyasu's edict of 1614 expelling all foreign priests and closing all churches. This resembled Hideyoshi's edict of 1587 in that it was not enacted immediately with any great severity, and no foreign priest perished during Ieyasu's lifetime. Boxer nevertheless describes the missionaries clearing all pictures and religious objects from their churches before the hand-over, and even going to the lengths of re-burying the bodies of their colleagues in secret locations so that their graves would not be profaned. Many priests, however, did not leave Japan, instead staying behind to minister in secret. This was the beginning of the 'underground church' of the *senpuku Kirishitan* (secret Christians). Boxer numbers these brave men at 47, plus a hundred *dōjuku* (Japanese lay catechists), and they were to be joined later by priests smuggled into Japan.[17]

The discovery that foreign priests were present in Osaka castle led Hidetada to strengthen his father's edict by another in 1616, although the accent was still on the expulsion of foreign clergy rather than the persecution of native Japanese Christians.[18] As the Japanese authorities had not quite grasped the difference between Protestant and Catholic, the English and Dutch traders were repeatedly questioned about their religious adherence. Cocks writes in 1617 that Hidetada's advisers 'sent unto me I think above twenty times to know whether the English nation were Christians or no'. Cocks had first answered simply in the affirmative, but in response to further questions he had hastily added that 'all Jesuits and friars were banished out of England before I was born'. This seems to have satisfied the authorities, and with the warning that if the English should communicate with the Portuguese 'they should hold us to be all of one sect', the English trading privileges were restored.[19] In fact, the Protestant sensibilities of both the Dutch and the English had long ensured that they were completely unsympathetic to Catholic Europe. Anti-Christian *daimyō* such as Matsuura Shigenobu behaved more charitably towards fugitive Catholic priests than did the avowedly anti-Papist Richard Cocks, who turned over to the Japanese

One way by which the secret Christians concealed their faith was by worshipping statues of the Virgin Mary disguised as Kannon, the Goddess of Mercy. This particular Maria Kannon is in Hondō on the Amakusa islands.

Three priests are rowed ashore in secret to minister to the Japanese Christians.

authorities a priest in hiding whose whereabouts became known to him.[20] Cocks' attitude is summed up by a passage in a letter he wrote on 17 February 1614: 'Here is reports that all the Papist Jesuits, friars and priests shall be banished out of Japan... but I doubt the news is too good to be true.'[21]

The underground priests had only a few years left to suffer the attentions of unsympathetic Englishmen, as rivalry between the Dutch and the English themselves, rather than Catholic against Protestant, eventually sealed the fate of the EIC's venture in Japan. Following the Anglo-Dutch peace agreement of 1619 there was some cooperation, manifested largely through joint attacks upon Spanish and Portuguese ships trading with the Philippines, a process that turned out to be more profitable than honest trade. From December 1621 serious consideration was given to closing the English factory in Hirado. The end came following the Amboyna massacre in 1623, when an English captain was tortured and executed on the grounds of having plotted to overthrow the Dutch garrison. As a result of this incident the EIC decided to concentrate its efforts on India, abandoning Japan.

SYSTEMS OF CONTROL

The year 1623 also saw the accession to the Shogunate of the third Tokugawa Shogun, Iemitsu. The underground priests held their breath lest the new broom would sweep cleaner than the old. As they had feared, Tokugawa Iemitsu (1603–51) was to prove more fiercely anti-Christian than either of his

The 'Christian cave' on the island of Wakamatsu in the Gotō group, where Christian believers met for secret worship.

predecessors, taking a curiously personal interest in the investigative procedures employed against those priests brought out into the light.[22]

The control that successive incumbents of the post of Tokugawa Shogun exercised against Christianity was but one aspect, albeit a very important one, of the control they endeavoured to exert over every facet of Japanese life. The ideology that lay behind the Tokugawa polity was Neo-Confucianism, which will be discussed later in 'The Ways of the Warrior'. For now we may note that any tension that existed between the ideas of ancient Chinese sages and the demands of the Tokugawa state were overcome by the reinterpretation and transformation of Confucianism itself. It was a familiar Japanese process, and the fact that it was used to control the one religious import that had not been willing to adapt shows how extremely the threat from Christianity was perceived.[23]

The order and stability that Neo-Confucianism cherished received its expression in the overall administrative machinery that successive generations of the Tokugawa refined. It was known as the *bakuhan* system, being composed of two elements: the central *bakufu* or Shogunate and the local government of the *han*, the *daimyō*'s fiefs. It is not surprising to see both these elements being brought to bear on the problem of Christianity.[24] In Iemitsu's time the control of the pernicious sect was undertaken largely at *han*-level through the office of the local *bugyō* (magistrate), who oversaw all legal matters together with the *metsuke* (censors), the 'all-seeing eyes' of Tokugawa Japan. The particular department covering these local religious affairs was known as the Shūmon aratame yaku (Bureau for the Investigation of Religion). The local inquisitors (a good analogy if not a direct translation) would examine cases brought to their attention where people were believed to have had transgressed from the Confucian demands of *kō* (filial piety) and *chū* (loyalty) by embracing a banned religion.

Confucianism may have provided a conceptual and administrative framework for controlling Christianity, but the actual policing function was given to the tame bulldog of Buddhism. Like every other institution in Tokugawa Japan, Buddhism was made to serve the state. In fact, it became its most humble and faithful servant: a status that was to cause it enormous problems in the reaction against the Tokugawa regime that followed the Meiji Restoration, 300 years in the future. During the 17th century, however, all Japanese, as households, were affiliated to a particular Buddhist temple. Though this was of itself nothing new, the *bakufu* institutionalized it on a national scale, giving the Buddhist clergy (and Shintō priests, because the Tokugawa regime recognized no practical distinction between the two) a policing function over the lives of their registered adherents with the overt aim of controlling Christianity. Under this *danka* system, the entire population of Japan was required to register at a *bodaiji* (family temple) within a defined geographical and social area. From 1671 the temples' bureaucratic duties were extended to cover the registration of births, marriages, adoptions, deaths, changes of residence and occupation.[25]

The anti-Christian element of the *danka* system became visibly apparent through the annual examination of the members of households, who were issued with a *tera-ukejō* (temple certificate) that confirmed that none of them were Christians. Until the Shimabara Rebellion, the *tera-ukejō* were issued only to former *Kirishitan* who had given up their faith, but following that upheaval, which had a markedly Christian nature, it was made universal.[26] The infamous Nagasaki *bugyō* Takenaka Umene, who occupied the post from 1626 to 1631, is credited with introducing a test for Christianity by requiring those under examination to show their rejection of the faith by the simple means of trampling on a Christian image. The ritual was called *fumi-e* (image trampling) a word also used for the Christian images set in wooden blocks with which the test was carried out. For non-Christians, stamping on the *fumi-e* eventually acquired the air of an annual ritual eagerly awaited as one event of the New Year celebrations, but to the *senpuku Kirishitan* the trial never lost its horror. Records show what the inquisitors were looking for: 'Old wives and women when made to tread upon the image of *Deus* get agitated and red in the face; they cast off their headdress; their breath comes in rough gasps, sweat pours off them.'[27]

Lacking the presence of an iconoclastic Protestant like Richard Cocks to tell them that all they were doing anyway was indulging in Papist idolatry, the *senpuku Kirishitan* had to suffer this annual denial of their faith. Yet they kept it up for generations, and having trampled upon a holy image, might then return to their homes and bring out from under the floorboards a similar image of Christ or His Mother. They would then bend the knee, and with no priest to hear their confession of such a public sin and grant them absolution, they would mumble an act of contrition, the words of which had been passed on as secretly and as faithfully as the image itself. Some secret Christians almost literally went underground in the sense of having as their churches and chapels the little store room round the back of their homes, which became the centre for worship and devotion in private groups. There they would gather, with an explanation already prepared about how the meeting was actually a village celebration with no Christian connections.

Should a secret Christian be revealed by the *fumi-e* process or any other, such as a raid on a house, the inquisitors could choose to bring about either death or apostasy. A Christian of the samurai class or a foreign priest might well be interrogated by Buddhist priests, among whose ranks were a few apostate Christians who pursued their calling with all the fervour of the convert. For a poor farmer or fisherman an immediate apostasy was expected as the simple reaction to the fear of death or the loss of livelihood. Torture helped the process along for either category, and Unzen, on the Shimabara peninsula, became the open-air torture chamber of the Nagasaki area. Nowadays Unzen is a popular hot spring resort, and most of its volcanic boiling water sources have been piped off into expensive hotels, leaving only one deep pool among its lunar landscape that still resembles the sight that met the eyes of its *Kirishitan* victims, who were either flung in or had ladles of scalding water poured over their lacerated flesh.[28]

One way by which Christian worship was concealed was to disguise the event as a village celebration. This is still maintained by the *Kakure Kirishitan*. Here we see members of the Yamada community on Ikitsuki at prayer within the home of their group leader during the Hattai-sama festival in 1995.

The aim of the torture was to make the Christians recant, because the authorities were astute enough to know that the blood of the martyrs was the seed of the Church. Apostates, on the other hand, could render a religion impotent from the damage they created. Inoue Chikugo-no-kami, who became the Tokugawa regime's 'Grand Inquisitor' when the Shūmon aratame yaku was centralized in 1641, was the master of this approach. Based in Edo with no volcanic waters in the vicinity, he specialized in the torture of *ana tsurushi*, which involved suspending the victim upside down in a suffocating, foul-smelling pit for days on end. A gash was made in the forehead so that the Christian would not lose consciousness. To this torture was added one mercy – the left hand was kept free so that a signal could be given that he or she wished to recant. So terrible was the torture of the pit that Inoue achieved one remarkable triumph by even forcing into apostasy one Portuguese Catholic priest: Father Christovão Ferreira.[29] The majority of native Christians did apostatize during these two decades, either through torture or the fear of it, but many of the resulting apostasies were, of course, as false as the apparent willingness to trample on the *fumi-e*. In 1637, 38,000 Christians appeared from nowhere to take part in the Shimabara Rebellion, and when searches were undertaken for secret Christians in the 1640s underground communities were found in all but eight of the Japanese provinces.[30]

RAIDS AND RETRIBUTION

The opportunity to demonstrate their non-Christian credentials, or even to make a false apostasy, was a privilege denied to those Christians who suffered one of the sporadic armed raids on suspect communities carried out during the 1640s. Such enclaves tended to be remotely located, such as the island of Ikitsuki to the north-west of Hirado.[31] The Ikitsuki 'Shōhō Persecution' of 1645 came about not from the vigilance of a nosy *metsuke* but from the suspicions of the chief priest of the Shūzenji, the temple at which the inhabitants of the southern part of Ikitsuki were registered. He reported to the *bugyō* that six of his adherents were probably underground Christians. All were executed, and as Ikitsuki already had a long history of Christian martyrdom going back to 1609, the *daimyō* in whose territory Ikitsuki lay (the second Matsuura to bear the name of Shigenobu) acted swiftly to eliminate the problem once and for all. A boat full of samurai from the island of Iki, who had no family connections with Ikitsuki, landed on the island under the command of a certain Kumazawa Sakubei. Kumazawa began the operation like a samurai general of old by praying for victory at the Shintō shrine of Hime-jinja, high on a bluff overlooking the harbour of Tachiura. He then began a systematic house-to-house search for any evidence of underground Christianity, such as printed or handwritten texts, rosaries or other devotional items, including ones disguised as Buddhist images. Anything that gave rise to the slightest suspicion led to a massacre of the inhabitants. Hundreds were killed.

Dotted around Tachiura are various memorials to the victims of 1645,[32] but not all the underground Christian homes could be reached easily on foot. One fisherman's hovel, now known as Danjikusama, could only be approached by boat. When the samurai landed there the family concealed themselves in a bamboo grove, but their baby's cries gave them away and they were put to death. Because of the way the massacre happened this place is revered by the fishermen of Tachiura, and once a year they visit Danjikusama to pray for large catches and safety at sea. But they always walk there. No fishermen in Ikitsuki will ever go to Danjikusama by sea.[33]

That Ikitsuki was to remain one of the most important locations of underground Christians for the next two centuries shows that the Shōhō raid was a failure, but this was not how it appeared to the brave general Kumazawa Sakubei, one of the few samurai for many years to have used his sword in anger. With that one massacre Matsuura Shigenobu II concluded that the work was done and reported to the Shogun that there were no Christians left in his territory at all.

That was the official version. We now know that they continued to pray in secret to something very secret indeed. Behind a pillar on the wall there may have been concealed a crucifix or a holy picture that only they knew was there. A potential source of embarrassment for the Matsuura appeared in 1658 when three *jabutsuzō* (evil Buddhas – the splendid name for disguised Christian statues) were discovered on Ikitsuki. The *daimyō* panicked, but fortunately for his pride the owner of the images trampled on a *fumi-e* and was released, thereby showing the joint characteristics of secrecy and denial that were to mark Ikitsuki Christianity for the next 200 years.[34]

It is important to note that throughout this time of persecution the underground witness in Japan was borne exclusively by members of the lower social classes. There were no underground *Kirishitan* samurai to defend them with their swords, nor any 'above ground' *Kirishitan daimyō* to plead for them in high places. Some *daimyō* may have shielded communities they knew to be Christian, but this would have been largely to avoid being punished themselves; actual believers at this level were the first to apostatize. The faithful Christian *daimyō* like Takayama Ukon had a bad habit of choosing the wrong side in wars where the Tokugawa were involved, and were now either dead or fled.

The sole examples of overt Christians still active in Japan were the Dutch traders in Hirado and the crews of the Portuguese ships who still called in briefly. Unlike the English, the Dutch do not seem to have helped the suppression of Christianity in any way, but neither did they promote it. If any secret Christians sought refuge with Dutch merchants then their secrets are

The site of a fisherman's hovel, now known as Danjikusama, marks the place of martyrdom for a Christian family on the island of Ikitsuki. A small shrine, much like a Shintō shrine, commemorates the family. The flags have been left by local fishermen as offerings.

concealed from history as well. On only one occasion was this policy of non-involvement challenged, when the Tokugawa Shogun called upon the Dutch in 1638 to assist him in suppressing the Shimabara Rebellion. The request had nothing to do with religion, and merely reflected the Shogunate's continuing lack of faith in Japanese-produced cannon, which had been demonstrated so clearly at Osaka.

The Shimabara Rebellion of 1637–38 was the only serious challenge to be mounted against the rule of the Tokugawa in two and a half centuries. The uprising began on the Amakusa islands and spread to the Shimabara peninsula to the south of Nagasaki. Having failed to capture the castle of Shimabara, the insurgents repaired the dilapidated castle of Hara that stood nearby, and held off the army of the Tokugawa for several months. Thirty-eight thousand people, most of whom were Christians, defended Hara under the command of a strange messianic figure called Amakusa Shirō.[35] Among the tactics used by the Tokugawa to reduce the fortress was a bombardment from ships anchored below the walls. The cannon were too light to do any damage, so the head of the Dutch factory in Hirado, one Koeckebacker, was first requested, then advised and finally ordered to send Dutch ships for service there. Even though the insurgents were Catholics who had damaged Dutch trade in the area by their rebellion, Koeckebacker displayed an admirable reluctance to provide ships and

The leaders of the Sakaime group of *Kakure Kirishitan* on Ikitsuki kneel in front of their altar at the start of the Easter celebrations.

artillery to destroy them. His first move was to send one of the two ships he had available off to Taiwan so that it could not be used. He arrived off Hara in the remaining *De Ryp* on 24 February 1638.[36]

Two Dutch sailors died during the operation. One was shot down off the top mast and crushed his fellow to death.[37] Ship to shore bombardment was then replaced by a makeshift land battery. During the 15 days that the Dutch were present at Hara they threw 426 cannon shot into it, so that, according to a Japanese source, the besiegers were required to 'build places like cellars, into which they crowded'.[38] The effect was therefore quite considerable, much greater than Koeckebacker either expected or acknowledged; however, he may well have played down the significance of his efforts because he regretted being forced into such a despicable act. One reaction by the besieged was to mock the Tokugawa army for having to rely on foreign help.[39] After two weeks the Dutch were thanked for their efforts and sent away prior to the final and bloody assault against the weakened castle that settled this last rebellion against the Tokugawa.

By the time of Shimabara the Shogunate may have grasped the distinction between Protestant and Catholic; but that consideration was less important in their eyes than the distinction between missionary and merchant. Portuguese ships were still trading with Japan while the rebellion raged on. All this was to change in 1639 with the *Sakoku* Edict. This important milestone in the relations (or lack of them) between Japan and Europe has commonly been regarded as one not of exclusion but of seclusion, whereby Japan adopted the policy of sealing itself off from the rest of the world until being 'awakened' by Commodore Perry's US fleet in 1854. Recent scholarship has called into question many aspects of *Sakoku*, showing that Japan was by no means totally isolated, as trade was still maintained with Korea and China. The one factor that is not disputed is the concentration of a policy of exclusion on Catholic Europe and the elimination of Christian influence. In this light, the non-existence of a secluded, isolated Japan makes the persecution of Christians appear even more severe than under the 'seclusion' model.[40]

By the *Sakoku* Edict Japan's Christian century came to an end. The helpful Dutch remained on Hirado, but in May 1641 they were suddenly and forcibly removed to Dejima. It was to become Japan's only window to the West for the next two centuries. The immediate Dutch reaction was one of resignation; however, the *Sakoku* Edict meant that they would be the only European nation still to be trading with Japan for the next two centuries, and this gave the cloud something of a silver lining. Although the Dutch were confined to their tiny outpost with a staff of only 27, during the 1640s the profit on the annual trade with Japan was over 50 per cent, making Dejima the Dutch East India Company's richest trading post.[41] Japanese copper was one of the elements of that trade, and silver soon became another commodity. In 1639 six ships from Japan had arrived in Taiwan with 3 million florins' worth of silver, and up to 1668 the stream of silver from Japan was an essential factor in the company's profits.[42] In 1647 a Portuguese embassy attempted unsuccessfully to re-open trade relations with Japan, explicitly stating that the regaining of access to the copper market was one of the main motives behind the move. The Portuguese had established very successful gun foundries in Macao and Goa, where Japanese copper had been used prior to the *Sakoku* Edict. It is interesting to note that cannon produced in Macao using Japanese copper were employed by the Duke of Wellington during the siege of Badajos in 1812.[43]

Mr Ooka, leader of one of the *Kakure Kirishitan* groups on Ikitsuki, kneels to pray in front of the holy pictures preserved and successively copied in secret for hundreds of years.

In 1673 England too tried unsuccessfully to re-open trade with Japan. The investigative mission brought along two brass guns and one mortar as presents for the Shogun, but the Dutch, who feared losing their monopoly, informed the Shogun that the English were in alliance with the Portuguese. This was not strictly true, but Charles II had a Portuguese queen, Catharine of Braganza, and that was enough reason for the ship to be turned away.[44] It was not until the founding of Hong Kong that the EIC came into contact with the Japanese again.[45]

Meanwhile the work of the 'Inquisition' continued, but by the beginning of the 18th century its tasks were becoming routine. In 1708 there was a flurry of excitement when Father Sidotti, the last in a long line of secret missionaries, landed in Japan and was immediately arrested. He died in prison in 1715. Following his death the Christians' prison was used for common criminals, then abolished altogether along with the 'Inquisition' itself in 1792, its work apparently completed. As far as everyone was concerned, Christianity had been totally eliminated from the 'land of the gods'. It was a century and a half before the true situation was revealed.

THE SHAKING OF THE FOUNDATIONS

The shaking of the foundations of the Tokugawa Shogunate began in 1854 with the arrival off the Japanese coast of an American fleet commanded by Commodore Matthew Perry. Not frightened away by the sight of armed samurai warriors glaring at them from the beach, the Americans landed, ending two centuries of Japan's self-imposed isolation. Trade negotiations followed. Ports were opened up and foreigners in strange, outlandish clothes began to walk the streets of Japan for the first time in two and a half centuries.

Among the foreigners allowed back into Japan were Catholic priests – not Portuguese Jesuits this time, but French missionaries who had studied the history of Christianity in Japan and its tragic extinction. The martyrs of Nagasaki had been canonized as recently as 1862, so Japan was in the forefront of Catholic thought. Missionary work among the Japanese was still out of the question – the churches that the priests were allowed to build were for the convenience of foreigners only – so the first concern with regard to the Japanese was simply to search for the descendants of the ancient Christians, 'whose existence they

In March 1865 in Nagasaki, Father Bernard Petitjean met a group of clandestine Christians at the door of his newly consecrated church in Oura. They were the first 'hidden Christians' to be discovered.

presumed'.[46] Such presumption had not dared to include the discovery of communities numbered in the thousands who were not merely descendants of the 'ancient Christians', but had kept the faith alive as an underground church for seven generations. Yet precisely this discovery was made, beginning in March 1865 in Nagasaki, when Father Bernard Petitjean met a group of clandestine Christians at the door of his newly consecrated church in Oura:

> Urged no doubt by my guardian angel, I went up and opened the door. I had scarce time to say a *Pater* when three women between fifty and sixty years of age knelt down beside me and said in a loud voice, placing their hands upon their hearts: 'The hearts of all of us here do not differ from yours.'[47]

The initial joy on discovering these communities soon gave way to two pressing practical needs. The first was to preserve the safety and anonymity of those discovered, because in the turbulent atmosphere that accompanied the Meiji Restoration a new wave of persecution had begun that would continue for 15 years until religious toleration was granted in 1873. The second requirement was to reconcile the underground believers' beliefs and practices with the teachings of the Catholic Church. This proved to be surprisingly difficult and in many cases impossible. The underground faith appeared to the missionary priests to be so riddled with Buddhism, Shintō and strange folk practices that its Christian element had all but disappeared. Nor did the attitude of the priests themselves help matters. They practised nothing of the accommodative method of the 16th-century Jesuits, and their rigidity provoked confrontation. The result was that while many 'hidden Christians' accepted conditional baptism and rejoined the Catholic Church, many thousands did not. As far as they were concerned, they had preserved the true teachings entrusted to them by Xavier and his followers. These people turned their backs on the new missionaries and stayed in their own faith communities. After 1873 they had no need to be *senpuku Kirishitan* any longer, but if not now exactly secret, they stayed separate, private and hidden from the outside world as Japan's *Kakure Kirishitan* (The Hidden Christians).[48]

THE HIDDEN CHRISTIANS

Several communities of *Kakure Kirishitan* still exist in the remote islands of western Japan. Their numbers have been dwindling for decades and it cannot be long before their ritual objects are displayed only in the museums of Christianity that have been set up on Hirado and Ikitsuki. Until then the private communities will continue to gather in their members' homes for rituals and worship that provide a valuable insight into the underground practices of

An *otenpesha* of the *Kakure Kirishitan*. This was originally a straw whip used for flagellation, but lost its significance during the time of secrecy and persecution, and is now used in much the same way as a Shintō priest's *gohei*.

the Tokugawa Period. One fascinating example of *Kakure* life is the sung prayers that are chanted during ceremonies. Professor Tagita, researching the *Kakure* in the 1920s, was the first man to study their prayers. He was told that the sung prayers were effectively nonsense syllables designed to confuse anyone who heard them chanting. Tagita transcribed what they had been singing to him and took the text back to the university. When he sat down and stared at it he realized that for the past 250 years, without knowing it, the Hidden Christians had been singing in Latin.

The *Kakure*'s blending of elements of Buddhism, Shintō, folk religion and Christianity into a syncretic expression, a process that horrified the French missionaries in the 1850s, now excites respect for the evidence it produces of how a Christian community, cut off entirely from the outside world, could preserve anything at all for two and a half centuries. Every worship session on their calendar ends with a communal meal. This has echoes of Shintō practice, but also reflects the need to conceal their activities from official investigation. The graves of their martyrs resemble Shintō shrines in almost all particulars, while certain holy objects have acquired new uses and significance. For example, one devotional practice recommended by the Jesuits was flagellation, so we find straw flagellant whips called *otenpesha* on the *Kakure* altars, although they are no longer used as whips but in a way similar to the Shintō priest's *gohei*, the paper wand with which blessings are given.

In some cases both the ritual and the object have changed so much that the combination has almost acquired a significance of its own. Rosaries would have been very incriminating objects if found during a raid. Nowadays we may find

A *Kakure Kirishitan* altar in a private house on Ikitsuki. On display are flasks of holy water, rosary beads and a paper cross called an *omaburi*.

a rosary on a *Kakure* altar. It may have been kept for centuries at great personal risk, or simply acquired early in the 20th century, but on Ikitsuki it is more common to note little crosses of white paper, because if anyone was suspicious of what was going on, you could pop it into your mouth and swallow it. The crosses (*omaburi*) are made during a special service and blessed by being sprinkled with holy water. Even the water has profound significance. Having no priests to make water holy for them, the underground believers of Ikitsuki obtained supplies from a fresh water spring on the tiny rocky island of Nakae no shima. This was the site of several acts of martyrdom early in the 17th century, so the association with the martyrs is believed to make the spring water, called *San Juan sama*, into holy water.

So far, so Catholic – but there is also a strong element of belief in evil spirits within the *Kakure Kirishitan* communities, and rituals exist to deal with them. In a number of rites practised on Ikitsuki, homes, fields and cowsheds are purified using some or all of the three holy objects just described. First the *otenpesha* is waved to chase away the evil spirits, then the area is cleansed using holy *San Juan sama* water, and finally an *omaburi* cross is left to ensure that the evil spirits do not return.[49]

Such rituals, of course, speak of Shintō and seem to disprove the claims the underground Christians made to the French missionaries that they were preserving the authentic teaching of the Jesuits. But were they so far from the mark? How well did the average 19th-century French prelate understand the religious world of the 16th century, where devils, demons and witches were believed to roam and had to be controlled? An examination of what people

The *Kakure* pantheon, which takes in Jesus, the Virgin Mary, saints and martyrs along with Shintō *kami*, is charmingly illustrated in this picture of the Annunciation, showing God, the Virgin, Jesus (already born!) and the angel Gabriel as a *tengu*. All these strange features are due to the total isolation the underground church experienced for over two and a half centuries.

actually believed and did in 16th-century Europe, as distinct from what the Church either said they did, or said they should have done, shows among other things that the uses of holy water went far beyond that of baptism and blessing. In 1623 parishioners in Brindisi were advised to keep holy water at home for 'chasing away demons and all their tricks'.[50] The pre-Reformation English parish clerk could earn a 'holy water fee' by sprinkling it on the hearth to fend off evil, and in cowsheds, fields and even on the marriage bed to ensure fertility.[51]

The sacred *mikoshi* of the Hime shrine on Ikitsuki is carefully guided down the flight of steps and between the shrine's *torii* gate during the annual festival.

But if the *Kakure* faith resembles 16th-century Catholicism in this respect, then it is very different from it in at least one other crucial aspect. This lies in the identification of the 'evil spirits' whom the *Kakure* rituals are designed to thwart. These evil spirits are certainly not the *kami* of Japan, who are instead respected and venerated in a *Kakure* pantheon that takes in Jesus, the Virgin Mary, saints and martyrs. This belief is in marked contrast to their 16th-century forebears, who performed rites of exorcism against evil spirits that on expulsion announced their true identity as Japanese *kami* whom the Christian God had driven from their thrones.[52] It was this total identification of the *kami* with devils that led to the ruthless destruction of temples and shrines by the first converts.

The survival of the underground church showed that, when there was no other alternative, Christianity could change in the Japanese environment – just as every other religion had done – even if the ultimate price was the mutual rejection of each other when the missionaries returned. Compromise had been necessary under persecution, and had to some extent come about naturally in the Japanese environment where, for example, non-Christians in a locality venerated sites of martyrdom like Danjikusama as the abode of powerful *kami*. This attitude made life easier for a hidden Christian who wished to remember his martyred relatives. The most moving illustration of this is the Hime-jinja shrine in Ikitsuki, the Shintō shrine where the general had prayed before going to massacre the inhabitants of the island in 1645. Every year they have a *matsuri* (festival), where they carry the *mikoshi* through the streets of the town, just like any Shintō festival anywhere in Japan. But this one has a strange feature to it, because it is taken through the *torii* of the martyrs' site of Sennizuka: 'the mound of the thousand dead'. The *mikoshi* is placed in front of the shrine of the martyrs and the priest kneels there and prays in front of them. This combination of a Shintō *matsuri* with a place holy to martyrs who were secret Catholics, which is now preserved by the separated *Kakure Kirishitan*, sums up another great truth about Japanese religion: that somewhere in the 'religious supermarket' there is a place for everyone.

One remarkable feature of the Hime shrine's annual *matsuri* occurs when the Shintō priest follows the *mikoshi* on to the site of Christian martyrdom known as Senninzuka, and prays there in front of the shrine.

在聖堂

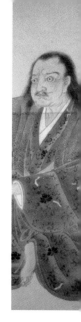

ZEN AND THE SAMURAI

Throughout this book the point has been made that the world of the samurai and the world of the sacred were not opposing entities. Instead, the two aspects coalesced into one unitary world view. To the Western mind there is no better evidence of this fact than the link that is frequently made between the samurai and Zen Buddhism. To many outsiders Zen *is* Japanese religion, and is therefore used to explain everything about the samurai from the battlefield to the tea house. This chapter will show that Zen does not provide the sole answer to 'what made the samurai tick', neither in art nor in warfare. Other influences contributed to the complex nature of the samurai's religious beliefs, and to the survival of the cultural legacy of the samurai and the sacred.

Zen Buddhism is by its nature a very confusing subject. Its origins may be traced back to the preaching of the historical Buddha, but not through any scriptures like the Lotus Sutra. Instead we are told that Buddha was once offered a flower and asked to preach the Law. He turned the flower in his hand but said nothing. All of his disciples were mystified, except one, the wise Kāshyapa, who realized the significance of the teaching, and was thereby entrusted with handing down a truth that could be transmitted without words.

Zen was taken to China by Bodhidharma, the 28th successor to Kāshyapa, during the 6th century AD.[1] Bodhidharma is known in Japan as Daruma, whose image is one of the most familiar depictions of a holy man to be seen anywhere in Japan today. Daruma spent nine years in meditation, and the effects this had on his physical state are expressed artistically by his appearance as a mystic wrapped in a cloak with wide open eyes and withered legs. His eyes stare

A striking depiction of the Zen patriarch Daruma on the wall of a temple in Hikone.

because he is said to have once fallen asleep and was so ashamed of himself that he cut off his eyelids.[2] Daruma also appears in this guise as a lucky doll. Traditionally you buy a Daruma doll with no eyes painted in, so you paint in one eye and make a wish. When the wish comes true you paint in the other eye. Darumas are very popular at the time of elections, and one imagines there are lots of discarded one-eyed Darumas after the votes have been counted.

The great pioneers of Zen in Japan continued this tradition of influence through a master who possessed a larger-than-life personality. The first Zen evangelist, Eisai (1141–1215), studied on Mount Hiei. On his return to Japan from China with the message of Zen he based himself in Kamakura, where his ideas (and his other Chinese innovation: the drinking of tea) found favour with the military government. But when Eisai moved to Kyōto he was forced to compromise with the established sects if his new ideas were to have any hope of taking root. Eisai's teachings became the Rinzai school of Zen, which made particular use of the *kōan*, a theme or problem the solution of which leads to sudden understanding. This moment of truth could be stimulated by some sudden dynamic revelation introduced by an external event – hence the familiar image of the Zen master striking his disciples on the back with a wooden stick.[3]

Eisai's willingness to compromise was in the great tradition of the accommodative world of the sacred in Japan, and it certainly helped the promulgation of his teaching. One characteristic of Zen has always been its adaptability; however, Eisai's successor Dōgen (1200–53) reflected the opposite

virtue of Zen by his rugged determination and uncompromising independence. This led to him leaving Kyōto for Echizen province, where he founded the Sōtō school of Zen. Instead of the Rinzai *kōan* being used to provide enlightenment, Dōgen stressed the practice of *zazen* (sitting in meditation) with no problem or goal in mind. The result would not be a sudden flash of awakening, but a gradual life-long realization. It was an attitude that could, and should, find additional expression through the performance of life's mundane daily tasks. A Zen monk raking the sand in a temple garden or a swordsman in a *dōjō* (practice hall) might both be expressing these very sentiments through their actions.[4]

Daruma is most often encountered in Japan as a lucky doll. Here is a collection of Daruma dolls waiting to be finished at a factory near Otsu.

The rapid growth of Zen is a remarkable instance of the wide-reaching developments that took place within Japanese Buddhism during the Kamakura Period. When Minamoto Yoritomo established his Shogunate in Kamakura there was not a single Zen monastery in Japan. In 1333 the members of the Hōjō regency ended the era by an act of mass suicide performed within a Zen temple, the Tōshōji, an institution that was then but one among many in Japan.

Why did Zen spread so rapidly? The usual explanation given for the popularity of Zen is the enormous appeal it had for the samurai. The word 'Zen' means meditation or concentration. Unlike other Buddhist sects, with their emphases on faith in Amida's vow or the seeking of enlightenment through study and ritual, Zen proclaimed that salvation was not to be sought outside oneself or in another world, because each person has an inner Buddha nature. Zen demanded discipline and emphasized self-understanding rather than hours spent studying texts. It also stressed intuition and action, and through its promise of enlightenment within this life rather than a world to come, a samurai was helped to face the prospect of death in battle with an attitude of detachment.

In an age threatened by the uncertainty of *mappō*, Zen offered a solution that was the complete opposite from the populist Amidist sects. Hōnen and Shinran taught that people could no longer help themselves (*jiriki*) but must be helped by another (*tariki*). Zen looked closer into the human soul than any other sect; so close, in fact, that it could demand great efforts on the part of its practitioners. In spite of Dōgen's praise for the 'daily round and common task', the monastery therefore provided its ideal setting, where only an elite few could pursue such a path. The samurai lay one step removed from the monastery, but turned to Zen because it offered them so much. This impression that Zen was very much 'in tune' with the samurai mind has given rise to the popular misconception that almost everything concerned with the samurai and the sacred can be explained completely by their espousal of Zen. From archery to garden design and from ink-painting to suicide, almost any topic can be considered under the by-line of 'Zen and the Art of…'. *Haiku* poetry, the Noh theatre, landscape gardening, flower arranging and the tea ceremony, let alone the entire canon of the martial arts, are all explained through the lens of Zen.[5] One eminent enthusiast describes this phenomenon in the following terms:

> When absolute cleanliness is a thing sought after, a Zen gardener may have a few dead leaves scattered over the garden. A Zen sword-player may stand in an almost nonchalant attitude before the foe as if the latter can strike him in any way he liked; but when he actually tries his best, the Zen man would overawe him with his very unconcernedness.[6]

Zen was undoubtedly attractive to the samurai mind, and some warriors are known to have practised meditation so assiduously that they were awarded certificates by Chinese masters.[7] One authority links the samurai class to Zen through the 'honest poverty', 'manliness' and 'courage and composure of mind' that they had in common.[8] But as this book has shown already, the contribution of Buddhism to the development of the samurai class within the Japanese 'religious supermarket' was much wider than could ever be encompassed within the teaching of one single sect, no matter how death-defying or manly that sect was. Also, many of the supposed exclusive precepts of Zen that are most often applied to the way of the samurai may be found elsewhere. For example, self-discipline lies at the very heart of Confucianism, and it was not just Zen practitioners who willingly accepted death in battle. Such fatalism was the *sine qua non* of the samurai warriors who fought in the Ikkō-ikki armies of Jōdo Shinshū. Even the *mikkyō* Buddhism of Shingon, with its mystical rituals and

secret transmission of doctrine, resembles Zen in its essential intangibility and its promise of enlightenment within this life. Shingon's painted mandalas, although very different in appearance from the understated brushwork of a Zen *sumi-e* scroll, provided a similar opportunity for insight into Buddha nature. Indeed, the continuing development of Zen after the fall of the Hōjō owes a great deal to the mingling of esoteric Buddhism with Zen in the person of an interesting character called Musō Soseki (1275–1351).

Musō Soseki studied Shingon Buddhism before entering the Zen priesthood and in 1325 became abbot of the famous Nanzenji temple in Kyōto. He was an important influence on the first Ashikaga Shogun, Takauji, and it was at Soseki's behest that Takauji established the *ankokuji* temples for the pacification of the war dead. When Soseki died his successor, Gidō (1334–88), continued to win friends and influence people. As an authority on Neo-Confucianism as

The famous Kinkakuji (Golden Pavilion) is a temple hall by the side of a lake in Kyōto. It was founded by Ashikaga Yoshimitsu, and represents a particular artistic tradition in Japan.

well as Zen, Gidō became the confidant of the great Shogun Ashikaga Yoshimitsu (1358–1408). Yoshimitsu was the 'renaissance prince' of Japan who not only brought to an end the schism in the imperial family, but also promoted trade relations with China (sundered because of the Mongol invasions) and patronized art and culture on a grand scale. It is to him that we owe the exquisite Kinkakuji (Golden Pavilion) in Kyōto. The present Kinkakuji is a replacement after its destruction by an arsonist in 1950, and its original form contained some remarkable interior features that expressed the syncretic nature of Japanese religion. The ground floor housed a statue of Amida Buddha. The next floor up had a statue of Kannon, the Goddess of Mercy, while the uppermost floor was a Zen sanctuary.[9]

ZEN, TEA AND THE GARDEN

The Golden Pavilion may be glorious, but in the quest for Zen aesthetics the earnest student tends to look elsewhere in Kyōto for something much more restrained, and finds it on the opposite side of the city in the Ginkakuji (Silver Pavilion). The Silver Pavilion was built by Yoshimitsu's grandson, Shogun Ashikaga Yoshimasa (1436–90), whose remarkable contributions to Japanese culture and Zen aesthetics were cruelly disrupted by the terrible Onin War of 1467–77, which reduced much of Kyōto to ashes and marked the curtain-raiser for the Age of Warring States. The situation of the times meant that no funds were available to cover the Ginkakuji in silver, so it remains to this day as a natural wood pavilion buried in the shadows of the hills of Higashiyama. It may actually have been Yoshimasa's intention to leave it in this modest state, because much of what we know as 'Zen culture' is enshrined here. The building represents perfectly the principle of *sabi* – the appreciation of that which is old, faded and rustic – and it exudes a lonely aura. It also expresses *wabi*, a more abstract concept that has to do with quietness and tranquillity.[10] Near to it lies the Tōgūdō, which houses a simple room that is considered to be the forerunner of the Japanese tea house. Finally, beside the Ginkakuji stretches one of Japan's most famous Zen gardens, although this was added during the 17th century and was probably not in the original design. An expanse of raked white sand with a raised cone said to represent Mount Fuji, it is said to look most beautiful in moonlight.

Related to *sabi* and *wabi* is the much older artistic principle of *yūgen*, roughly translatable as 'mystery'. In art there is *yūgen* in the achievement of a simple perfection and a perfect simplicity. As 'a suggestive indefiniteness of vague and therefore of spiritual effect', art produced under the spirit of *yūgen* hints at things rather than stating them plainly. The Noh theatre is the greatest example of *yūgen* in action, or rather in inaction, when a moment of stillness rather than of gesture conveys something very profound.[11] Once again one must not rush to the conclusion that *yūgen*, *wabi* and *sabi* are exclusively the property of Zen. All had their origins long before Zen came on to the scene. Seami (1363–1443), the great master of Noh, took existing artistic values and both transformed and enhanced them through the influence of Zen. What was 'charming' in the Heian Period became 'moving' in the Muromachi Period. But even if Zen is recognizable in the expression of the Noh theatre, there is much more than Zen Buddhism to be found in the content of the plots of its plays. These strange tales of ghosts and tragic victims contain strong elements of folk religion and a longing for rebirth in the Buddhist Pure Land. Shintō *kami* also play a prominent role, so the Noh theatre may be regarded more as an expression of the syncretic blending of Japanese religious and artistic traditions both in its form and function.[12]

A much closer association with Zen may be found in *chadō* (the way of tea). Of all the pastimes in which a samurai could indulge none had more lore and tradition associated with it than the performance of the tea ceremony. Tea had originally been introduced to Japan as a means of keeping Zen monks awake for their nocturnal devotions. In addition to its ubiquity as a beverage, however, tea drinking developed in this one highly specialized way that encompassed much of what a samurai valued in terms of aesthetic appreciation and sensitivity. The way of tea centred on the drinking of a bowl of green tea with like-minded companions in an artistically pleasing and aesthetically inspiring manner. The ceremony would take place in a tea room, which was often located in a tea house set within a tea garden. The décor of a tea house was traditionally very simple and rustic in accordance with the principles of *wabi* and *sabi*. The guests would enter from the garden and take their places, after which the tea master, who was sometimes a *daimyō*, would join them through a separate door made deliberately low so that the tea master was forced to express his humility by crouching down. A meal of exquisite design and quality might be served, but the centre of the meeting was always the tea ceremony itself, whereby the master boiled the water and served the tea in a strict formality that allowed his guests to appreciate every gesture and factor involved. They would admire the quality of the pottery used in the vessels, the artistic depiction of the seasons in a flower

This simple gateway into a tea garden in Hirado represents perfectly the principle of *sabi*: the appreciation of that which is old, faded and rustic and exudes a lonely aura.

A performance of a Noh play within the shrine of Itsukushijima on the holy island of Miyajima. The actor is silent, expressing through mime the emotions that accompany the chanting and music.

arrangement or a hanging scroll and the play of light in the garden outside, partially visible through the sliding screens. Most of all they would be enthralled by the motions of the tea master as his hands moved in a 'kata of tea' that would be reminiscent of the greatest exponent of swordplay.

Where the tea ceremony left Zen behind lay in the uses, or rather abuses, the samurai made of it. Hideyoshi, whose flamboyance in artistic matters was renowned, was known to have used a tea room where the wooden beams were plated with gold, and the political pay-offs from the tea ceremony were similarly outrageous. Information gathered from guests, political support confirmed by attendance, bonds of comradeship forged by fellow enthusiasts, gifts of priceless tea bowls and other earthly benefits arose from these gatherings. Murder might even be plotted over a nice cup of tea, and on two occasions at least murder was almost carried out. The tea master Sen Rikyū is said to have fended off a sword stroke using his tea ladle.[13] Katō Kiyomasa once went to a tea ceremony hosted by a rival whom he wanted out of the way. He hoped to find the man so engrossed in the ritual that Kiyomasa would be able to stab him with a spear. But the man's deportment was so alert and in control that Kiyomasa never caught him off guard.[14] Nothing could be further from the ideals of Zen, but then Katō Kiyomasa would have had no dealings with Zen anyway, being an exclusivist of the Nichiren persuasion.

Even when the tea ceremony was being performed with all the punctilious exactness that Zen demanded, its socially competitive potential should not be overlooked. The way of tea sorted the aesthete from the boor and distinguished

A set of masks for a performance of Kagura, a primitive version of Noh, at a shrine festival in Shimobe.

the patient man from the over-hasty. It revealed areas of self-control that would stand a samurai in good stead both in a *zazen* session or on the battlefield. As a tool of 'personnel selection' it exposed his weaknesses under pressure. In the tea ceremony a samurai practised the inner martial arts where he had no sword but his wits, and no defence to a challenge but to draw on the fund of aesthetic knowledge he was required to possess.

Many anecdotes exist that relate skill in the tea ceremony directly to skill on the battlefield. Ueda Shigeyasu was mocked by younger retainers in his lord's service, who concluded that his exquisite performance in the tea house meant that he would exhibit an opposite level of skill in battle. In 1615, however, Shigeyasu led Asano Nagaakira's vanguard at the battle of Kashii, one of the important preliminary actions of the Summer Campaign of Osaka, and took an enemy head:

> Standing up before the whole assembled clan, Shigeyasu exclaimed, 'How now you fellows? You have derided me as a tea-page of ten thousand *koku* and declared that my sword would only be wet with the blood of a cat or a mouse, and how has it turned out? You, who have never known anything about tea, but only have devoted yourselves to martial arts alone, are not only less distinguished than a Tea Master like myself, but have done practically nothing at all!'[15]

Many of the Zen temples and monasteries that nowadays make Kyōto such a fascinating and inspiring place to visit owe much of their appeal to their exquisite gardens. Even if these gardens express ideas that go beyond Zen, it is

In the background is the tea house of the Tōji-In in Kyōto set within a pond garden designed by the Zen master Musō Soseki.

undoubtedly true that the philosophy behind Zen Buddhism provides for them the perfect spiritual home. One particular feature of these gardens is their asymmetry, an artistic principle that derives from Taoism as much as it does from Zen. In *The Book of Tea* Kakuzo Okakura recognizes this dual debt:

> [Taoist and Zen philosophies] laid more stress upon the process through which perfection was sought than upon perfection itself. True beauty could be discovered only by one who mentally completed the incomplete. The virility of life and art lay in its possibilities for growth. In the tea-room (as in the garden) it is left for each guest in imagination to complete the total effect in relation to himself.

In another passage Okakura advises the artist to leave something unsaid so that the beholder is given the chance 'to complete the idea. Thus a great masterpiece irresistibly rivets your attention until you seem to become actually a part of it. A vacuum is there for you to enter and fill up to the full measure of your aesthetic emotion.'[16] So in a *kare-sansui* (dry landscape garden), where a cleverly arranged system of rocks and sand suggests a mountain gorge, every element is present except water. The essence of Zen in this situation lies in the beholder not merely imagining the water, but himself becoming the water.

Even in a garden layout there is always more present than just Zen ideals. Taoism is noted as an influence above, and what considerations, one wonders, lay behind the selection of the particular rock that occupies a prominent position in the spectacular garden of the Sambō-In at the Daigōji temple in Kyōto? The rock, known as the Fujito, is beautiful enough in its own right, but its chief claim to fame is that it was chosen because its surface was stained by the blood of a samurai killed during the Gempei War.

The *kare-sansui* (dry landscape) garden of the Taizō-In within the Myōshinji complex in Kyōto. This little garden is a Zen invitation to the viewer to 'add the water'.

ZEN AND THE MARTIAL ARTS

Japanese aesthetics clearly owe a debt to Zen in many aspects of their expression, but just as in the more narrowly 'religious' world of the sacred, it is the blending of different but complementary elements into a satisfying whole that provides the final picture. Is the same true of the martial arts of Japan? Is Zen their bedrock, as it is often claimed to be?

An examination of the written sources can be quite confusing. The extraordinary claims made for the purity of the styles of sword-fighting *ryūha* (schools), for example, can daunt even the boldest scholar. The admirably

This simple hand basin in the Ryōanji garden is an item that expresses so well the mystery and aesthetic beauty of Zen.

RIGHT

In the tiny Daisen-In garden in Kyōto's Daitokuji these huge rocks provide the cliffs for an imaginary roaring torrent that flows through the garden in a symbolic representation of the journey of life.

undaunted Karl Friday has tackled this topic head on, and it is interesting to note that his study of one of Japan's foremost sword-fighting traditions, the Kashima Shinryū, is concerned with an organization that cannot be linked exclusively with Zen. Indeed the reverse is true. Its founding is associated firmly with Shintō tradition, while Kamiizumi Nobutsuna, the school's great exponent, took a keen interest in Zen as did his famous student Yagyū Muneyoshi. Other master swordsmen down its genealogical line embraced Pure Land Buddhism, and Friday begins his book with a quotation from a Confucian scholar.[17]

Nevertheless, many fine contemporary written works exist that link Zen and swordsmanship in a convincing manner. For example, *Fudochi Shinmyoroku*, by the Zen priest Takuan Sōhō, who taught Zen meditation to the great swordsman Yagyū Munenori, has as its essence the concept of *fudochi* (permanent wisdom). This means that the working mind, though constantly changing, is always attached to nothingness, and therefore to the eternal universe. In this view Zen Buddhism takes swordsmanship directly to the goals of attaining enlightenment and the achievement of selflessness. By the blending of self and weapon through action the swordsman moves towards that complete emptiness which is the aim of all Zen practices.

One must always bear in mind, however, that most of the written material about Zen and swordsmanship was produced at a time when the art of the samurai swordsman was not encumbered by any need actually to win battles. By being thus concerned with means rather than ends, sword-fighting entered the realm of the meditation on daily things that would have been so valued by Dōgen. When samurai were real fighting men the value they attached to Zen could be very different. The 'means' provided by *zazen* was an excellent 'training for the mind', and would therefore be a very valuable preliminary exercise for the fight. But the samurai existed to serve his master, and numerous accounts emphasize that a samurai should never waste his life needlessly. Actively seeking death on the battlefield or simply throwing one's life away in a street brawl was condemned as an unnecessary deprivation of the service one rendered to one's lord.[18] The Zen 'detachment' of popular myth was therefore a means of preparing a man for death, not an encouragement towards seeking it.

Because of the master/servant relationship in which he found himself – a relationship that owed more to Confucian ideals of hierarchy and filial piety than it did to the essential independence of Zen thought – a samurai's life was precious, and a Kamakura samurai could not escape from the constraints that

Other considerations beyond Zen led to the selection of the Fujito rock in the Sambō-In garden, because its surface is stained with the blood of a samurai killed during the Gempei War.

The Zen priest Takuan Sōhō, who taught Zen meditation to the great swordsman Yagyū Munenori, from his statue in Yagyū village.

this relationship placed upon him. Nor could the art of swordsmanship escape from this bloody reality until a time when it no longer had to be used primarily for killing people. Before the Tokugawa Period very few swordsmen were able to lift the art of the samurai sword on to a higher philosophical plane. The men who succeeded were the *kengō* (master swordsmen) like Miyamoto Musashi who went on 'warrior pilgrimages' (*musha shūgyō*). This was much akin to the common Japanese practice of making long religious pilgrimages to distant parts, thereby obtaining spiritual enlightenment through endeavour and personal discomfort.[19]

The typical 'sword pilgrim' was likely to have had some service to a *daimyō* and some battle experience behind him before setting off. His wanderings could last for several years, and might include temporary spells of military service and some teaching. Austerity and abstinence were the hallmark of the pilgrim warrior, whose travels would invariably involve duels, each of which taught the swordsman a little more about himself. In the Age of Warring States *kengō* were much in demand as teachers to a *daimyō*'s retainers, but with the coming of peace even cowards could sometimes pass themselves off as experts. Every desk-bound samurai bureaucrat was theoretically a sword-fighter, and as Friday notes so perceptively, 'it would have been as unthinkable for a samurai to confess to complete unfamiliarity with his swords as it would for one of his contemporaries in New England to confess to total ignorance of the Bible'.[20]

In the hands of a master the practice of the martial arts acquired a genuine spiritual dimension and became a process of self-realization in which Zen played a vital role. Nor was there any separation made between the practical and physical on one side, and the philosophical and spiritual on the other. Just like the blending of Japanese religion and daily life, they were seen as a continuum of martial experience in which various religious traditions merged.[21] Yet there are still martial arts practitioners who wish to lay claim to their territory exclusively in the name of Zen. This is best illustrated by the most controversial link of all between the samurai and Zen through the practice of *kyūdō* (Japanese archery). The position may be summarized by the following quotation:

> The purpose of Zen archery is not to hit the target, but rather the concentration achieved by the archer in order to create a style that expresses his perfect mental serenity. When the archer does hit the centre of the target in such a state of mental calm, it is proof that his spiritual discipline is successful. The spirit (*shinki*) is linked to the target by the union of man, bow, and arrow, and ultimately this linkage achieved through strict mental and physical discipline produces a personal character that blends harmoniously with life… In fact, *kyūdō* without any reference to Zen is a meaningless exercise.[22]

This is a considerable claim to make, but how realistic is it for the age of war? Archery was a fundamental skill of the samurai until the introduction of firearms in the 16th century led to a shift in emphasis with missile weapons from targeted sharp-shooting to mass infantry tactics. The samurai of the Gempei War referred to their calling as *kyūba no michi* (the way of horse and bow) and skill at archery was much more highly prized than skill with the sword. At this time every archer certainly intended to hit the target – his life depended upon it, let alone the fundamental demands of service to his master – so any philosophical or religious ideas that he applied to his military prowess would be subservient to those vital considerations.

Modern *kyūdō* (archery) in action, a martial art that is associated too closely in the popular mind with Zen.

The above quotation is from a modern work that derives from a very influential book called *Zen in the Art of Archery*, written by Eugen Herrigel in 1953.[23] Herrigel enjoyed several 'mystical' experiences in the presence of *kyūdō* practitioners, including a rather eccentric teacher of his own, and interpreted them through his own views of Zen. As 'a credulous enthusiast who glorified Japanese culture', he let his imagination run riot when it came to analysing the relationship between what he saw and what he believed lay behind the events.[24]

The reality is that in Japan *kyūdō* was only to be associated with Zen after the time of Herrigel, not before. This is not to say that Zen had no influence on archery. An early Tokugawa Period manuscript concerned with archery quotes from a Zen text of 1229, but only in the context of the mental attitude

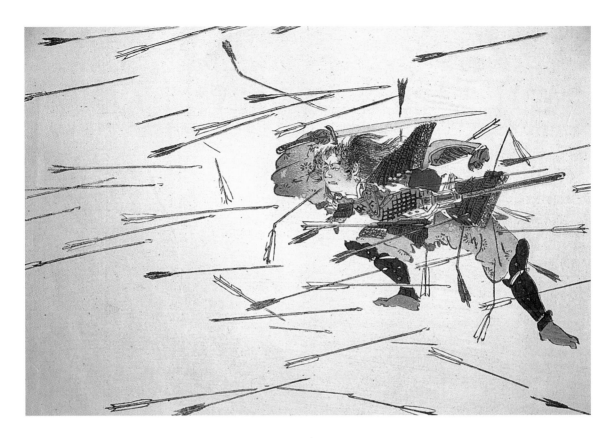

of samurai, because 'When one is willing to sacrifice oneself and regards lightly the loss of one's own life, then one's bow comes alive.' Yet in this very same paragraph there is an additional reference to Shingon concepts,[25] so once again we see an example of Japan's 'religious supermarket' in action.

In conclusion, Zen was a very important influence on samurai culture, but it was not the whole story, and this can be seen best by its failure to explain one other well-known concept concerned with the samurai and the sacred: *bushidō* – the way of the warrior. This is the topic to which we will now turn.

A samurai is met by a hail of arrows. This was the reality of Japanese archery during the time of war, and owed nothing to Zen Buddhism other than a determination by the samurai to face death bravely and with a composed mind.

THE WAYS OF THE WARRIOR

Just as Shintō means 'the way of the gods', so does the well-known expression *bushidō* mean 'the way of the warrior'. There is a strange parallel between the emergence of the two terms. The word 'Shintō' was introduced to provide a label for something that had been going on for centuries and had required no name until it was felt necessary to distinguish it from something else. As noted earlier, scholars are divided as to whether this happened when Buddhism was introduced, or when the founding fathers of the Meiji government sought to create a new ideology. *Bushidō* has a similarly confusing genesis. No event was more important to its creation, development and dissemination than the publication as late as 1905 of a book called *Bushido: The Soul of Japan*, written in English by Inazo Nitobe. It carries the subtitle 'an exposition of Japanese thought', and is widely regarded as a classic, particularly by people who have not actually read it.[1]

As attested by its century-long catalogue of reprints, its translation into numerous languages and its enthusiastic reception by Westerners and Japanese alike, no book has been more influential in making the ideas and ideals of 'the way of the warrior' accessible to the outside world. *Bushido: The Soul of Japan* stimulated the publication of other works. One year after its arrival an English translation appeared of an autobiographical work that seemed to confirm everything that Nitobe's book stood for. In *Human Bullets* a Japanese soldier tells how he made up his mind to sacrifice his life in battle, because 'I was fully determined to die this time.'[2] This was Nitobe's thesis translated into stirring and chilling action, which gave it the blessing of authenticity.

OPPOSITE

The archetypal image of *bushidō*: a samurai fighting bravely among a fall of cherry blossom.

153

Bushido: The Soul of Japan is a very curious work. Its author was born in 1863, but was shielded from the turbulence of the Meiji Restoration, first by the education he received in schools where the main medium of teaching was in English, then by the Christianity he espoused and to which he remained dedicated all his life, and finally through a certain physical isolation in Hokkaidō. The result was a highly literate scholar with a keen sense of internationalization, whose immersion in a Western education of the English public school variety (often referred to as 'muscular Christianity') was equalled only by his stunning lack of knowledge of Japanese culture.[3] This would not have mattered had he not produced a book about Japan that was to become an international bestseller outside Japan and a cornerstone of right-wing nationalism within it. That is what happened, however, and although he willingly admitted his ignorance over vital topics such as Zen Buddhism ('so far as I understand it...')[4] Nitobe's book, with its strange blend of samurai myths and *Tom Brown's Schooldays*, became regarded as the bible of *bushidō*.

Central to Nitobe's presentation of *bushidō* as the 'warrior's code' is his identification of seven key values: justice, courage, benevolence, politeness, veracity, honour and loyalty. In the same way that critics of Shintō's official line of history readily acknowledge the pre-existence of *kami* worship, so it must be recognized that all these virtues were present in Japan in pre-Meiji times. All indeed are splendid ideals that would first have graced the halls of a *daimyō*'s castle and then transformed his sword-wielding samurai into brush-wielding exemplars of Tokugawa society. Where Nitobe exceeded his brief was to assume that they made up a rigid 'warrior's code' called *bushidō*. Nitobe presents *bushidō* as a code that was ancient and universally adhered to by the samurai, who effectively swore to obey it like a version of the Hippocratic Oath. Such was the popularity of Nitobe's work that not only was all this fully accepted, but his other misconception – that *bushidō* was a moral force that had become in modern times 'the soul of Japan' – became true by default as a self-fulfilling prophecy. In an age that actively sought fundamental values for a rapidly changing society, Nitobe's thesis was exactly what early 20th-century Japan wanted to hear. In 1908 Itō Hirobumi included the word in his *Reminiscences on the Drafting of the New Constitution*:

> The great ideals offered by philosophy and by historical examples of the golden ages of China and India, Japanicized in the form of a 'crust of customs', developed and sanctified by the continual usage of centuries under the comprehensive name of *bushidō*, offered us splendid standards of morality, rigorously enforced in the everyday life of the educated classes.[5]

Thirty years later *bushidō* is mentioned several times in *Kokutai no hongi* (Fundamentals of Our National Polity), the high-water mark of Japanese

A single combat with swords: the ideal role of every samurai, but one that was not often performed, even during times of war.

nationalistic writing. It was first published in 1937, and 2 million copies were eventually printed. By this time the devout Christian Inazo Nitobe had been dead for four years, and one wonders what he would have made of the following section:

> *Bushidō* may be cited as showing an outstanding characteristic of our national morality. In the world of the warrior one sees inherited the totalitarian structure and spirit of ancient clans peculiar to our nation. Hence, though the teachings of Confucianism and Buddhism have been followed, these have been transcended. That is to say, though a sense of obligation binds master and servant, this had developed into a spirit of self-effacement and of meeting death with a perfect calmness... It

155

Katagiri Katsumoto, one of the 'Seven Spears of Shizugatake', in mounted combat during that famous battle in 1583.

is this same *bushidō* that shed itself of an outdated feudalism at the time of the Meiji Restoration, increased in splendour, became the Way of loyalty and patriotism and has evolved before us as the spirit of the imperial forces.[6]

Prior to Nitobe, a wide range of expressions – all meaning 'the way of the warrior' – may be found in the literature, such as *shidō* and *budō* (the first syllables are the same as in *bushidō*). But where the actual term *bushidō* appears the meaning is always that of a general attitude rather than a rigid accepted code known to all. Nitobe's book does, however, make it clear that *bushidō* was less concerned with the individual samurai than with the relationships the samurai had with others, of which the most important was that between master and follower. One of the finest expressions of this relationship comes from Torii Mototada, who wrote a last letter to his son in 1600 prior to the fall of Fushimi castle, which he had defended so valiantly for Tokugawa Ieyasu:

> For myself, I am resolved to make a stand inside the castle, and to die a quick death.
> It would not be difficult to break through the enemy and escape... But that is not

The reality of *bushido* lay not in any seeking of death, but in the relationship of service between a samurai and his master, as seen in this scroll in Matsuyama castle.

the true meaning of being a warrior, and it would be difficult to account as loyalty… to show one's enemy one's weakness is not within the family traditions of my master Ieyasu. It is not the way of the warrior to be shamed and avoid death even under circumstances that are not particularly important. It goes without saying that to sacrifice one's life for one's master is an unchanging principle.[7]

Torii Mototada sees his conduct as being in keeping with the tradition of service to the ideals of the Tokugawa family, rather than being driven by a code. He goes on to remind his son of their family and its relationship with the Tokugawa, referring to the 'benevolence' of their lord and the 'blessings' they had received at his hands. It is this relationship that is the key to his behaviour, not some abstract philosophical principle.

That Torii Mototada's master recognized his own obligation in giving benevolence is shown by the document that the first Tokugawa Shogun left for the instruction of his followers. The *Tōshōgū goikun*, effectively 'The Testament of Tokugawa Ieyasu', was first published during the reign of his grandson, the third Tokugawa Shogun, Iemitsu. In language curiously reminiscent of the Chinese

Toyotomi Hideyoshi, who inspired fierce loyalty, here plays the *shō*, a wind instrument like pan pipes, as his troops move into action at the battle of Shizugatake in 1583.

concept of Heaven's Mandate, the Tokugawa had been divinely entrusted with ruling Japan in the way of heaven (*tendō*), but if that rule were exercised badly the mandate could be withdrawn. To Ieyasu the 'way of the warrior' had been since ancient times the means by which the Shogun had purified the realm of evil. The quality of *chūshin* (loyalty) was the virtue required of inferiors, while their leaders responded with *jihi* (benevolence), which was the hallmark of a peaceful and just government. In a curious analogy made with the Japanese crown jewels, the three cardinal virtues in achieving a harmonious outcome were wisdom, the principle of the mirror; benevolence, the principle of the sword; and straightforwardness, the principle of the jewel.[8]

CONFUCIANISM AND THE SAMURAI

One of Tokugawa Ieyasu's retainers, Okubo Tadataka, wrote a book in 1622 called *Mikawa Monogatari*, where he acknowledged that Ieyasu's triumph in re-establishing the Shogunate was due to the close spiritual cohesion he had achieved between a lord and his followers. This system of mutual dependence was retained as the samurai moved from the battlefield to civil administration, and became a fundamental element in Tokugawa rule.[9] Not surprisingly, such a tight system of ethics did not come from nowhere, and central to this master/follower relationship were the teachings of Confucius. In Confucian eyes good government was based on virtue and example rather than on sheer military might, and was expressed as a balance between the two sacred entities of the nation and the family. Just as the father was head of the family, to whom was due the obligation of *kō* (filial piety), the Shogun was the head of the nation, to whom was due also the obligation of *chū* (loyalty).

Strictly speaking, the 'official theology of the Tokugawa regime' was not Confucianism but Neo-Confucianism.[10] Neo-Confucianism had been created as a response to the dominance of Taoism and Buddhism in China around the time of the Song Dynasty by scholars such as Zhu Xi (1130–1200), who felt that Confucianism lacked a metaphysical system and proceeded to give it one. Neo-Confucian influence was present at the start of the Tokugawa Shogunate, either as the orthodox Zhu Xi school (in Japanese *shushi gaku*), or the views of Wang Yangming (1472–1529), who stressed one's everyday behaviour rather than the mere investigation of things or legitimating of status. The quest for the crucial innate knowledge, according to some of Wang Yangming's followers,

An image of Confucius inside the hall of the Nagasaki Confucian temple, housed since its destruction by fire in 1959 within the Zen Kōfukuji in Nagasaki.

was best served by meditation that would bring intuitive enlightenment, a process that had much in common with Zen. Other interpretations of Wang Yangming stressed *shisei* (acting out of sincerity) a notion that would become the lever for rebellion in the later Tokugawa Period.[11]

As Confucian adviser to Tokugawa Ieyasu, Hayashi Razan reckoned that 'those who are adept at the handling of troops regard the arts of peace and the arts of war as their left and right hands'.[12] His role was to assist Ieyasu, the man of war, to become a man of peace as well, and to crown his military success with the achievement of an enduring social order based on Confucian ethics, where the samurai cultivated the arts of peace and devoted themselves to Confucian learning. Other scholars were less idealistic, seeing their role primarily as a challenge to find something for the unemployed samurai class to do. In his book *Taiheisaku*, Ogyū Sorai (1666–1728) denounced what he saw as the bad behaviour of his class, both on duty and off, writing, 'perhaps they believe that the mere acquisition of their professional skills, martial arts, is the way of the warrior'.[13]

Yamaga Sokō (1622–85) agreed that there was more to the way of the warrior than prowess at martial arts. He was a follower of Wang Yangming, and was also an early advocate of the importance of studying Western warfare and equipment, a need that was only recognized at a national level two centuries later. Sokō was profoundly concerned with the need to find a new role to replace the now unnecessary one of fighting battles. He believed that the samurai had to serve as a model for society, serving his lord with exemplary devotion and with no thought of personal gain while displaying the traditional samurai values of austerity, self-discipline and readiness to face death. The umbrella terms he uses for these ideals include *shidō* (the way of the samurai) and *bukyō* (the warrior's creed), for which *bushidō* is often loosely substituted, although nowhere does Sokō imply the rigid warrior's code envisioned by Nitobe.[14]

Whatever the gloss placed on his words, Sokō was wise enough to recognize the difficulty of applying those ideals to the days of peace, but if he had survived three decades more he would have seen a classic instance of the principles he espoused being put into operation. This is the well-known story of the Forty-Seven Rōnin, whose revenge killing in 1702 amazed contemporary Japan.

RELIGION AND THE RŌNIN

The loyal 47 samurai were retainers of Asano Naganori (1667–1701), who was based in the town of Ako (now Banshū Ako) in Harima province. In 1700 Asano, together with a certain Kira Yoshinaka, was commissioned to entertain envoys of the emperor at the court of the Shogun. Kira Yoshinaka held the office of 'Master of Ceremonies', and it was the custom that his colleague should give him some presents in order to get instruction from him and thus avoid any error of etiquette. When Asano brought no gifts Kira, deeply offended, spared no opportunity to scorn his colleague. One day Asano lost his temper, drew his short sword and wounded Kira on the forehead. Even to draw a weapon in the presence of the Shogun was a very serious matter, so Asano was arrested. He was ordered to commit *seppuku*, and actually carried out the act the same day that he had attacked Kira.

The Shogun added to the agony by deciding that the territory of Ako should be confiscated as punishment. By this act Asano Naganori's retainers were to be made unemployed and dispossessed. They would become *rōnin* (masterless samurai, literally 'men of the waves'), and it was at this point that they decided to avenge their dead lord. The chief retainer Oishi Yoshio Kuranosuke retired to Kyōto, where he began to plot a secret revenge with the 46 others. The blanket of concealment they wove was to become the most famous characteristic of the vendetta. Kira Yoshinaka feared that there might be a plot against him, but his spies only found men apparently addicted to drink and given to pleasure.

近松勘六源行重
三十四歳

大高源五源忠雄
三十二歳

On a snowy night in December 1702, Asano's retainers took a surprise revenge on Kira at his mansion in Edo. The guards were taken by surprise, the doors were broken in by huge mallets, and a fierce swordfight ensued. Oishi Yoshio cut off Kira's head and placed it on Asano's tomb in the Sengakuji temple in recognition that a solemn duty had been fulfilled. They also left a written address to Asano:

> we, who have eaten of your food, could not without blushing repeat the verse, 'Thou shalt not live under the same heaven nor tread the same earth with the enemy of your father or lord,' nor could we have dared to leave hell and present ourselves before you in paradise, unless we had carried out the vengeance which you began.[15]

Two of the celebrated Forty-Seven Rōnin, whose revenge killing stunned contemporary Japan. This scroll is in the Oishi shrine in Banshū Ako.

One of the *rōnin* had been killed in the raid, so it was the remaining 46 who went to the authorities and proclaimed what they had done. The government had thus been placed in a nice quandary. The samurai of Ako had fulfilled their moral duty but had broken the law, and, theoretically at least, law and moral duty could not come into conflict in Tokugawa Japan, because both were based upon the Tokugawa 'state religion' of Neo-Confucianism.[16]

The first consideration dealt with the legality of their vendetta. Even in a society that valued the notion of revenge, a man was not entirely free to do as he liked, and there had emerged during the 17th century a system of registered vendetta called *kataki uchi*. If a deed was committed that required avenging, the avenger was required first to present a complaint to his own *daimyō*, from whom he would get authorization to search for and slay the enemy.[17] The existing precepts did not actually allow for avenging the death of one's lord, only a relative. That was the first complication for the Ako samurai. The second problem was that their vendetta depended totally upon launching a surprise attack on the well-defended Kira, so registration would have been impossible anyway.

The decision the government reached was that the law must be upheld at all costs. The possible consequences of giving official approval to an unauthorized vendetta were too ominous to contemplate, so the *rōnin* were ordered to commit *seppuku*, a course of action for which they had been prepared from the start.[18] In spite of the adulation heaped upon them by later generations, the reaction from one of their best-known contemporaries was unenthusiastic. A passage in *Hagakure* criticizes the Forty-Seven Rōnin:

> After their night attack, the rōnin of Lord Asano made the mistake in failing to commit *hara kiri* at Sengakuji. Furthermore, after having let their lord die, they delayed in striking down his enemy… These Kamigata types [i.e. from central Japan as distinct from sophisticated Edo] are clever and good at doing things that earn them praise,… but they are unable to act directly without stopping to think.[19]

The author clearly preferred an act of revenge to be carried out in a death frenzy 'without stopping to think', rather than slowly, carefully planned and in secret, but Yamamoto Tsunetomo, the author of *Hagakure,* was something of an 'armchair samurai'. He was a retainer of the Nabeshima *han*, and when his lord died he wished to follow him in death (*junshi*). Being frustrated in this, Tsunetomo retired and produced *Hagakure* (Hidden Behind Leaves) – the archetypal samurai manual published in 1716. In it we may detect something of Tsunetomo's despair; first,

A Japanese businessman burns incense before the graves of the Forty-Seven Rōnin in the Sengakuji in Tokyo.

that the peaceful days of the Tokugawa Period made it impossible for him to live like a true samurai, and second, that the laws against *junshi* enacted by the Tokugawa prevented him from dying like one. *Hagakure*, with its famous sentence proclaiming that 'the way of the warrior is found in death', was his therapy, and it is more than a little ironic to hear him criticizing the Forty-Seven Rōnin in its pages. In an age when samurai were government employees whose loyalty, once expressed so dramatically on the battlefield, had become reduced to turning up for work on time, both he and they were glorious anomalies. Far from being typical samurai of the age, the loyal retainers of Ako became famous because they were so different from almost all their contemporaries.

Later generations came to idolize the Forty-Seven Rōnin, and one commentator wrote, 'from scholars, ministers and gentlemen down to cart pullers and grooms, there is no one who does not slap his thighs in admiration'.[20] Although they were officially criminals, they could still be worshipped as *chūshin gishi* (loyal and dutiful samurai), who sacrificed their lives for a transcendent cause.[21] Once the Tokugawa were safely out of the way the Forty-Seven Rōnin could be safely honoured at a higher level, and in their own little way they contributed something to the Meiji polity. One of the first acts of the new Meiji emperor was to send a message to the Sengakuji:

> Yoshio, you and the others resolutely grasped the righteous duty binding a lord and
> his vassal in exacting revenge and then greeting death according to the law. Even a
> hundred generations later, people are still inspired by your deeds. I wish to express
> my deep appreciation and praise to you.[22]

By this endorsement the Meiji government further repudiated the legal and religious judgement of the hated Tokugawa whom they had replaced. Yamaga Sokō's teachings, which had provided the inspiration for the Forty-Seven Rōnin, had also been promulgated by Yoshida Shōin, one of the great martyrs of the restoration movement. Apart from settling this score, the Meiji government would go no further in honouring the Ako samurai. Because the wounding of Kira had occurred during the visit of an imperial messenger, to some extent the Ako affair could be seen as insulting to the emperor.

A shrine to Oishi Yoshio and his companions was founded in their home town of Banshū Ako in 1912 and became a further place of pilgrimage along with the Sengakuji in Tokyo. In an incident that transcended religious beliefs, Zen had played no part in the revenge of the Forty-Seven Rōnin other than the coincidence that the place where Kira's head was taken was a Sōtō Zen temple. Confucian ideas of filial piety and benevolence on the one hand and loyalty on the other were the motivations that drove them forward, and there was no argument as to where their duty lay in this classic blending of the enduring traditions of the samurai and the sacred.

THE EMPEROR'S NEW CLOTHES

The Meiji Restoration gave Japan more than new rulers. It provided unique challenges that arose from the interaction between tradition and modernity. To one foreign commentator at least, it also provided a new religion:

> The new Japanese religion consists, in its present early stage, of worship of the sacrosanct Imperial Person and of His Divine Ancestors, of implicit obedience to Him as head of the army (a position, by the way, opposed to all former Japanese ideas, according to which the Court was essentially civilian); furthermore, of a corresponding belief that Japan is as far superior to the common ruck of nations as the Mikado is divinely superior to the common ruck of kings and emperors.[23]

This is quite an acute observation, as the military upheavals of the restoration period were to be followed within a few years by further incidence of conflict, when the same founding fathers sent Japanese troops to fight in foreign wars. These soldiers were not samurai but conscripts, and the introduction of conscription challenged many values in Japanese society. Former samurai families greatly resented having to mix with lower classes.[24] Farmers resented the disruption that conscription caused to rural life when simple country boys, whose ancestors had been forbidden from carrying weapons by Hideyoshi's Separation Edict, suddenly became soldiers. The introduction of conscription even provoked riots among people to whom the ideals of the defunct samurai class meant nothing.

The challenge faced by the government was quite considerable. Somehow this disparate entity called the Japanese army had to be made to perform on the battlefield in the spirit of the samurai of old, and it was uncomfortably clear that such commitment did not come naturally to the majority of their fighting men. Conscription had destroyed forever the traditional bonds of loyalty that had existed between a samurai and his *daimyō*. These values may have become almost meaningless except in extreme cases like the Forty-Seven Rōnin, but what was there to put in their place? Some of the officers in the new Japanese army may have been descended from samurai, and lugged ancestral swords into battle as a link to their ancestors' honourable past. But this would not work for the common soldiers who now constituted almost 95 per cent of the Japanese armed forces.[25] They needed something on which they could focus their loyalty to the point of death. The solution, of course, was for them to concentrate their patriotic spirit on the emperor, to whom the conscript swore absolute loyalty on enlisting. Just as the samurai had once repaid the 'debt' for the 'benevolence' shown to him by his lord with a display of self-sacrificing loyalty, so now was the entire population of Japan placed in a similar situation of debt simply by being born as a subject of the emperor.

To the background of cherry blossoms, the eternally poignant symbol of the samurai, Toda Ujikane points his war fan in the direction of the enemy. He is wearing a typically practical suit of armour embellished by a lavish helmet with a large *maedate* (helmet crest). This statue of him is outside Ogaki castle.

The emphasis laid right from the start on the willingness to sacrifice one's life for the emperor implies that such an extreme demand came no more naturally to a Japanese fighting man than it did to a soldier of any other nation. How far could the ordinary man ever identify himself with the samurai ideal set out in *Hagakure*?

> Meditation on inevitable death should be performed daily. Every day when one's body and mind are at peace, one should meditate upon being ripped apart by arrows, muskets, spears and swords, being carried away by surging waves, being thrown into the midst of a great fire, being struck by lightning, being shaken to death by a great earthquake, falling from thousand-foot cliffs, dying of disease or committing *seppuku* at the death of one's master. And every day without fail one should consider himself as dead.[26]

The answer would appear to be 'very little', so the world of the sacred was brought in to bolster the failing values of the world of the samurai. For example, during the Sino-Japanese War of 1894–95 Buddhist army chaplains served on the battlefield just as their predecessors had done centuries before. Many of the priests came from the Pure Land sect based at Nishi Honganji, and were to return to the battlefield when Japan went to war against Russia in 1904. During that conflict their leader, Otani Kōzui, sensed a duty and a responsibility that went far beyond the immediate spiritual needs of the dying soldiers:

> The Russo-Japanese War is the most important event of our times, upon which depends not only the survival of our country, but of our religious sect as well... Therefore we should devote ourselves to aiding in this war not only to protect the nation but to protect the Buddhist faith... If Japan loses the war and is forced to come under the control of the Russians, we cannot expect them to tolerate the existence of Buddhism...[27]

As Pure Land believers the Honganji priests naturally reassured the dying that they would be rescued by the *nembutsu* and go to the Pure Land, but their words to the living went far beyond Buddhist assurances and personal psychology. It was a deliberate attempt to foster and support the 'spirit of Japan' (*yamato damashii*), constantly reiterated through exhortations about the need for patriotism, reminding the soldiers that this was expressed above all through devotion to the emperor. One sermon reads, 'Dying in war is honourable... So soldiers must win, win, and win, even if it means holding on to the last rock, and serve the emperor and people to ease their anxiety.'[28]

Otani's wartime efforts did not go unheeded, and in 1912 he was personally thanked in a note from the Meiji emperor, whose name had been on the lips of the dying soldiers who had done their duty. But the achievement of an honourable death in war was difficult to reconcile with the tragic reality of the battlefield and the loss of friends and family. So, instead of providing a means of accepting death, the common religious behaviours associated with joining the army and then living within its demands expressed more of a desire to avoid death. Prayers at shrines were offered for survival rather than for glorious extinction, and the carrying of shrine amulets provided a personal

Kannon, the Goddess of Mercy, appears above the battle as the *kami kaze* pilots attack the American fleet. From a mural in the Kamikaze Museum in Chiran.

psychological and religious assurance. Some amulets became renowned for their power to 'avoid bullets'. One private's account describes his feeling of 'divine protection':

> I was lucky to have escaped injury in the three battles in which I had to take part, and am very happy and satisfied… I am convinced that it was because of the divine protection from the gods and buddhas, and am very grateful to them.[29]

But if these ideals of willingness to die for the emperor failed for the ordinary conscript of 1904, surely there is evidence of their successful acceptance during the final months of Japan's greatest conflict, when suicide pilots dived their planes into the flight decks of American carriers? The suicide pilots even chose a name for themselves that linked them directly to the destruction of the Mongol invaders by the *kami kaze*. Some authors are under no illusion that the *kami kaze* were the ultimate expression of the samurai ideal. In *The Japanese Cult of Tranquillity*, von Durkheim compares the state of mind of the *kami kaze* pilots to that of a Zen monk 'who knows when his hour has come'. To him the *kami kaze* were the supreme expression of the true Japanese outlook:

> To speak of their performance in such terms as 'patriotism', 'idealism', 'youthful dedication', or 'heroism' is to misjudge them entirely. These pilots, in risking death, proved that a form of human death does exist in the midst of life… There is a manner of dying which transcends the antithesis 'life and death'…. He has attained perfect tranquillity…[30]

What is most interesting here is that in seeking the answer to the state of mind of the *kami kaze*, von Durkheim goes back far beyond the Meiji Restoration and its patriotism to the vocabulary of *Hagakure*, where, in its most famous phrase, 'the Way of the Samurai is found in death'.[31] At first sight, the letters and diaries of the *kami kaze* pilots would appear to confirm this view. They indeed appear to have attained the state of tranquillity that was essential before setting off on the final mission. That their deaths had meaning was one comfort as they shrouded their natural human impulses in a protective cloak of acceptance. The giving of branches of cherry blossom bearing the eternal symbol of the samurai, the fastening of white headbands round the forehead and the drinking of a final cup of *sake* before leaving were all tiny rituals that linked their acts to the ancient samurai tradition: 'To die while people still lament your death; to die while you are pure and fresh; this is truly *bushido*. Yes, I was following the way of the samurai… I would fall "as pure as the cherry blossom."'[32]

Passages like this remind one of the continuity of the relationship between the samurai and the sacred. There is the same appeal to precedent that was expressed on board Shigenobu's ship in 1592, evidence that within this self-selected elite the

Angels carry a dead *kami kaze* pilot to heaven in a mural in the Kamikaze Museum in Chiran.

ideals of the samurai could provide the means to transcend the natural human fears that mundane religious rituals and appeals to patriotism never seemed to achieve.

A similar attitude is to be found in a later 'self-selected Japanese elite' of the so-called 'Red Brigade' terrorists of the early 1970s. These men provided a Japanese example of the violent world-revolutionary terrorists of the times, and 'contributed' to the cause of the Palestine Liberation Organization (PLO) by spraying machine-gun bullets at Lod Airport in Israel in 1972. Yet even in such a bizarre international act of cooperation the spirit of the samurai was not far from their minds. The confessions of their leader reveal that when they were training in Lebanon 'they would finish their after-dinner grenade-throwing with a session of moon viewing'.[33]

There is much more of a religious dimension apparent in the acts of a more recent coterie of 'sacred Japanese warriors'. In March 1995 a religious cult called Aum Shinrikyō, which had begun its existence as a yoga and meditation group, embraced mass murder when it released poison gas on a Tokyo subway train. Investigation into the incident revealed a sinister version of one of Japan's 'New Religions' that was controlled by a charismatic figure who had moved from a quest for universal salvation to an acceptance of a symbolic battle between good and evil. As the group retreated from the world this battle became less and less purely symbolic and more and more real, culminating in the death of its own followers along with many innocent people.[34] Nothing could have been further from the ideals of *bushidō*: the essential but elusive way of the warrior.

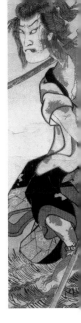

FROM SAMURAI TO SPIRIT

The birth pangs of modern Japan began during the last few years of the Tokugawa Shogunate when conflict arose over the future of Japan. The opening up of the 'closed country', forced upon the Shogunate by the arrival of Commodore Perry's fleet in 1854, was a development that was far from welcome to many in Japanese society. Whereas the supporters of the Shogun cooperated with the Western nations by signing treaties and promoting trade, their opponents believed that his acquiescence to Western demands was a sign of weakness and a betrayal of traditional Japanese values. The perceived threats that this posed also brought out into the open many dissenters who had been dissatisfied in general terms with other policies followed by the Tokugawa family over the years. These people had their own ideas of how to face the new dangers posed by foreign nations, and soon came to believe that the main obstacle hindering the expulsion of the 'barbarians' was the continued existence of the Shogunate, which should be replaced by the restored rule of the emperor. Political opinion was profoundly divided, and was backed up by terrorist acts from both sides of the argument. Modern Japan was therefore born out of years of feuding and tension when samurai swords found many victims.

The actual Meiji Restoration began late in 1867 when a newly formed army of conscripts together with the more traditional samurai forces of the *han* of Satsuma and Chōshū captured Kyōto. The Shogun accepted defeat and tendered his resignation. In January 1868 diehard supporters of the Tokugawa attempted to recapture the city but were heavily defeated at the battle of Toba-Fushimi. This was the beginning of the Boshin War, during which the imperial army

OPPOSITE

A dying samurai stands transfixed with a sword through his neck. This ghastly image sums up the horror of the 'Realm of the Beasts' that was the Japanese battlefield.

171

marched on Edo, where they captured the ex-Shogun without bloodshed. The city was renamed Tokyo (the eastern capital) and became the seat of the new Meiji government, although fighting continued in the north of Japan until 1869. Meanwhile, the new Meiji government instituted many reforms in what is usually portrayed as a largely peaceful process of embracing the new: a time of hope when enthusiastic and progressive samurai eagerly replaced their top knots with top hats. However, the breathtaking speed of the growth in international trade, the development of railways, commerce and communications hid numerous internal contradictions and conflicts to which the world of the sacred was far from immune.

In spite of all the modernity that it enthusiastically embraced – much of which, it must be said, was originally inspired by a desire to make Japan strong enough to withstand foreign powers in a possible war – the Meiji Restoration was born out of something that was of itself very ancient and very Japanese: the idea that the emperor would rule over a Japan that was at one and the same time a modern country and a semi-divine, paternalistic and authoritarian state. The emperor could certainly embrace modern technology – indeed he must –

Akechi Mitsuhide, who usurped Oda Nobunaga in a treacherous attack in 1582, but was soon defeated at the battle of Yamazaki. Here we see him in hiding, exhausted and wounded, receiving comfort from a loyal retainer inside the bamboo grove from which he will shortly emerge to face his death.

but his kingship by right of descent from the Sun-Goddess owed nothing to Western ideas of monarchy and even less to Western ideas of divinity. Shintō ideas had inspired those who had brought about Japan's great change, and Shintō would benefit most from them in religious terms. As explained earlier, Christianity caught the backlash of this viewpoint. What is more extraordinary is the way in which Buddhism was hit by the full force of resurgent Shintō, ensuring that the Japanese world of the sacred would never be the same again.

THE RESURGENCE OF SHINTŌ

At the time of the Tokugawa regime's founding, Shintō had been at a low ebb. The *kami* were honoured by ritual as they had always been, but Confucianism provided the model for government and Buddhism acted as its loyal and subservient means of social control. Even Shintō priests and their families had to register at their local temple, just like everyone else in Japan, and they were almost always forced to have Buddhist funerals, a matter that caused great resentment. Buddhist priests inevitably held higher positions than Shintō clergy, who could do little about it because many shrines were subordinate to a temple. The theological and pastoral role of the shrine/temple complex was in the hands of the Buddhist clergy. Shintō priests had roles that hardly went beyond liturgy, as they served the needs of popular devotion to the *kami* for rewards that were of a 'this-worldly' nature. They had no particular doctrine, and no need of a professional priesthood.[1]

Shintō ideas experienced something of a revival during the 18th century through the growth of *kokugaku* (national learning): a movement that examined the ancient history of Japan on the basis of the Japanese classics. Its pioneers came to reject Confucian and Buddhist opinions in favour of Japanese virtues. Motoori Norinaga (1730–1801), to whom Shintō was a fully fledged Japanese religion, was to produce the classic definition of *kami* cited earlier. Hirata Atsutane (1776–1843) became a passionate spokesman for the purification of Shintō from Buddhist and Confucian influences and mercilessly criticized Ryōbu Shintō. The Tokugawa regime did not agree, and silenced him for the last few years of his life.[2] *Kokugaku* was eventually to provide the intellectual and political background for the Shogunate to be overthrown in the name of imperial restoration.

For the whole of the Edo Period Buddhism served the Shogun as his faithful lapdog, and as long as the Shogunate survived, Buddhism's future was secure. When the Tokugawa fell from power Buddhism was forced to stand on its own as an institution and had to survive without special privileges. It was then that the backlash began, at a governmental level, an intellectual level and from anyone in the population who saw the opportunity to settle old scores.

With the ideology provided by *kokugaku* to propel them along, the reformers of Meiji Japan turned their attentions towards purging Shintō of its Buddhist 'impurities'. As has been noted so often in this book, the two were so thoroughly mixed that they were practically inseparable. The Great Shrine of Ise provides a striking example of the fusion of the two traditions at the time of Meiji. Though it was Japan's holiest Shintō establishment, by 1868 nearly 300 Buddhist temples existed in its immediate vicinity. The recitation of Buddhist sutras in front of altars of the *kami*, who were believed to be in need of these prayers to attain salvation, was fully accepted, and many Buddhist priests travelled to Ise on pilgrimage. Even the imperial family were affiliated with a Buddhist temple – the Sennyūji in Kyōto – and there was a special room in the palace for the family's *butsudan* (Buddhist altar). This was done away with in 1871 and the *ihai* (funerary tablets) sent to the Sennyūji.[3]

Yet this apparent religious harmony conceals a great tension that lay beneath the surface. In their prayers at Ise Buddhist priests were, perhaps unconsciously, reasserting an enduring authority over the native gods that had originally been bestowed upon Buddhism by the Nara court. Every resolution of the *kami* versus Buddha problem had resulted in the *kami* being relegated to an inferior position. It was always the gods of Japan that were in need of salvation, not the other way about. To this was added the Tokugawa Shogunate's use of Buddhism as a means of social control and the position of Shintō priests as 'second-class citizens': a situation that was to be completely reversed by a government decree of 28 March 1868 to enforce *shinbutsu bunri* – the separation of Shintō and Buddhism. What actually happened was the expulsion of Buddhism from long-established Shintō/Buddhist sanctuaries. This was often accompanied by violence and the destruction of property as a thousand years of syncretism came to an end.

The Omiwa shrine, described earlier because of its holy mountain, provides an excellent illustration of the decree's devastating effects. The place had always had extraordinarily deep ties with the imperial family. Both the *Kojiki* and the *Nihon shoki* state that the mountain's *kami* was a manifestation of the great *kami* of Izumo,[4] while the syncretic ideas of Ryōbu Shintō identified the mountain and its *kami* as being of one body with Amaterasu and Dainichi Nyorai.[5] Such a glorious coexistence meant that up to the Meiji Restoration Omiwa had three *jingū-ji* (shrine/temple complexes), of which now only a single structure remains. Following the fateful decree of 1868 the Buddhist monks in Omiwa's temples were forced to become Shintō priests. The temples' treasures were removed and orders were given for the demolition of most of the structures that housed them. The largest of the three temple complexes, the Byōdōji, was completely destroyed in 1870, leaving the Omiwa shrine in the 'pristine' Shintō form of shrine and mountain that so moves visitors today. Yet none of this history is mentioned in the modern literature published by the shrine. As far as

these publications are concerned the identification of Mount Miwa as the *shintai* of the *kami* and the mountain's long-lasting holiness is all there is to say. Centuries of Shintō/Buddhist accommodation were wiped out to make way for the new 'traditionalism' required by Meiji Japan.[6]

As well as purging existing Shintō shrines of any Buddhist colouration, the Meiji reformers systematized them and controlled the form of activities their newly liberated priests could undertake. Shintō funerals were encouraged, and an attempt was made to replicate the Tokugawa *danka* system by requiring all households to register at a Shintō shrine. Both these innovations proved unpopular, lasting only two years. Furthermore, when the government was faced with protests at the attacks on Buddhism, which in some cases had gone much further than the government had either ordered or wanted, the Shintō reformers began to think again. What they came up with was even more extraordinary than the forced separation of Buddhism and Shintō. Realizing that the immediate 'Shintōization' of Japan was impossible, the Meiji regime created an artificial designation that they called State Shintō, a non-religious or super-religious cult applicable to the adherents of all religions. The Constitution of 1889, which guaranteed religious freedom for the first time, was not intended to exclude any Japanese subject from participating in the rites of State Shintō, which had as their focus the ideals of national morality and a fierce patriotism through devotion to the emperor. All shrines were classified and graded into a hierarchy.[7]

The Otani cemetery in Kyōto contains thousands of graves holding ashes of the deceased.

The government also created several new shrines, of which the best known is Japan's famous, and to many people notorious, Yasukuni shrine, built to honour the nation's war dead. As the controversy over the meaning and significance of the Yasukuni shrine is such a complex one, we must first examine the whole issue of death and the warrior.

THE SAMURAI WAY OF DEATH

Throughout samurai history great store was laid on the example set to a warrior by the glorious deeds of his ancestors. A successful samurai would revel in his deeds of valour not just for himself but for the contribution he had made to a long-standing family tradition. This emphasis upon the household (*ie*) rather than the individual is an important characteristic of Japanese religious belief. There are Confucian elements here, with the emphasis upon *kō* (filial piety) as the basis of an ordered society. As the samurai obsession with pedigree shows clearly, the emphasis did not end with the death of a family member. The most important way in which the primacy of the family is expressed in Japanese religion is ancestor worship, whereby the structure of social relationships within the family unit is extended to encompass the dead. Japanese ancestor worship, which is not a separate religious sect but a series of beliefs integrated into the overall religious system, ensures that death does not extinguish a person's involvement in the life of his family. Instead, by a complex series of rituals designed to keep the ancestors peaceful and content in the successive stages through which they will pass, this continuity is assured.

Lined up with a very un-Japanese symmetry, the graves of the Mōri family lie within trees in the city of Hagi.

In early Japan the dead were treated with a mixture of fear and respect. The corpse was of course a major source of pollution that required Shintō rituals of purification, but the spirit of the dead person was also frightening because it could linger in the realm of the living. In a vivid metaphor, the spirit at the time of death had 'sharp edges' and still retained a strong individual personality. If the proper rituals were not carried out the spirit could become unhappy or even unruly. If the process was done properly it gradually lost its sharp edges and became 'as smooth as marble', eventually losing all its individuality as part of the collective spirits of the locality.[8] The spirits of the dead were therefore venerated and, to some extent, manipulated, along the journey they had to take in order to become ancestral *kami*.[9]

The process of guiding the spirits of the dead was carried out through the rituals of Buddhism, and was such an important practice that there was a gradual yet significant shift in the interpretation of what salvation actually entailed. Less emphasis was placed on the salvation of the living and more on the salvation of the dead. Many people came to regard 'funerary Buddhism' as the main religious function of the Buddhist clergy. This attitude persists today[10] and clearly illustrates the blending of Buddhism with native Japanese beliefs, as the most striking feature of the syncretic process is that when a person dies he 'becomes a *hotoke* (buddha)', a concept contrary to orthodox Buddhist thought. Furthermore, the process of enshrining a spirit does not fit in with traditional Buddhist beliefs in reincarnation, which taught *inter alia* that the Ten Kings of the Underworld passed judgement on each person's spirit after death as to which of the six realms of transmigration the spirit should be born into.[11] A further contradiction is found with Jōdo Shinshū, whose followers maintain that the believer's spirit leaves the world immediately for the Pure Land.

For the first 49 days from death the aim is to separate the spirit both from the corpse and from the world of the living. Two temporary *ihai* (memorial tablets) of unlacquered wood or paper are made. One is left at the grave site, the other is taken away from the cemetery and placed on a low table in front of the *butsudan* in the home. The *butsudan* may be an elaborate affair like a miniature version of the altar in a Buddhist temple. The temporary *ihai* is replaced on the 49th day by the permanent *ihai* of black lacquered wood on which the deceased's posthumous name is written in gold. The deceased person will be addressed through the *ihai* – very important objects known to have been rescued at great personal risk from burning buildings as if the ancestors lived in the tablets.[12] In 1615 one samurai rode into battle with a giant 2m-high (6ft 6in) *ihai* fastened to the back of his armour to show his acceptance of death. It was no doubt with similar, although diametrically opposed views of their worth, that led to their *butsudan* and *ihai* being gleefully burned or thrown into the sea by the Jesuits' first Christian converts.

The daughter of a family near Nara prays during the festival of Bon, the annual event to welcome back into the household the spirits of the dead; as it is the first Bon since the death of her grandmother, well-wishers have presented the paper lanterns seen here.

The separation of the spirit from the body is only regarded as complete on the first Bon (the festival of the dead) following the death, the annual event in August when all the ancestral spirits are welcomed back into the household. Springtime cherry blossom viewing, with its timeless association with the brief lives of the samurai, was once an occasion for welcoming returning spirits of the dead, and this persists in some communities.[13] The return of the spirits provides a further example of the intangible quality of the Japanese spirit world:

The world beyond cannot be described in any but equivocal phrases. Spatially it is both here and there, temporarily here and now. The departed and ancestors always are close by, they can be contacted immediately at the household shelf, the graveyard or elsewhere. Yet when they return 'there' after the midsummer reunion, they are seen off for a great journey. They are perpetually present – yet come and go from periodic household gatherings.[14]

For the next three or four decades the ancestors will be addressed through their *ihai* and remembered through various forms of prayer and services. Memorial services for the dead continue to be held until either the 33rd anniversary of death or possibly the 50th anniversary, depending upon the tradition, when a final service is held and the spirit of the ancestor becomes a *kami*. At this time the *ihai* is supposed to be deposited in the temple. The ancestral *kami* now remain eternally in the land, and continue to work for its prosperity and that of the family, but at this stage the various ancestral spirits have not yet become one. When they come back at Bon, they come back as the ancestors of the village, and each goes to his own family as its ancestors. This process is regarded as continuing as long as there is living memory within the family, after which the ancestral *kami* must be treated as a collectivity.

The ancestors who have been treated appropriately through the years of remembrance outlined above are a benign, friendly presence. If the sequence is neglected, however, the spirits of the dead may become unhappy in the afterlife. What happens to the dead who have no one to mourn for them? They are known as *muenbotoke* (buddhas of no affiliation). *Muenbotoke*, lacking the support of relatives during the period of transition, fail to become part of any family's collectivity of ancestors. From this perspective they are to be pitied rather than feared,[15] and food may be left for them when they return at Bon, although the offerings are made outside houses rather than in a family home.

THE REALM OF THE BEASTS

Further complications arise when a person dies a violent or untimely death, and thus 'remain possessed by the worldly passion in which they died'.[16] It is 'vengeful spirits' (*goryō shinkō*) or 'angry ghosts' (*onryō*) such as these – often dead samurai slaughtered on battlefields – that provide rich material for the numerous ghost stories and plays that make up many Noh and Kabuki dramas. The battle of Dannoura in 1185, which ended so tragically for the Taira, was to result in almost an entire family of unhappy spirits roaming the earth searching for revenge.

The needs of battle victims for funerals *in situ* provided a valuable role for the Buddhist priesthood. This was a charitable duty adopted in particular by monks of the Jishū (Ji sect), which derived from the Pure Land preaching of the priest Ippen (1239–89). The name means the 'time sect' because of its members' practice of reciting the *nembutsu* for six hours of the day. Unusually among founders, Ippen was descended from a samurai family: the Kōno, who had been one of the principal naval powers in the Inland Sea. Ippen used dance to spread his word, and his exuberant joy at the assurance of rebirth in paradise proved to be so great that when he first led his congregation in a dancing *nembutsu* the wooden floor collapsed.[17] Having had no desire to found a new sect, Ippen burned all his books and writings before his death, so the resulting Ji sect is best regarded as a branch of Hōnen's Jōdo sect. Prominent *jishū* (the same name was used for its members) were involved in cultural affairs such as flower arranging, but they are best known for their role on the battlefield.

Battlefield *jishū* priests, who were effectively Buddhist army chaplains, would tell stories and recite poems during lulls in the fighting, and could also be counted on to perform funerary *nembutsu*. They might even advance at great risk to their own lives during the midst of battle to offer *nembutsu* to the spirits of those who had just died. Dying soldiers would also be given the assurance of salvation. According to a letter sent by the chief priest of the Ji sect's Yugyōji near Kamakura, when the Hōjō were defeated at Kamakura in 1333 the battlefield resounded with repeated *nembutsu* cries and prayers uttered by samurai on both sides under the kindly influence of the *jishū*.[18] *Jishū* also provided memorial services, and would perform the useful act of visiting relatives of the slain and reporting deeds back to the home temple.[19]

A fascinating account of *jishū* in action comes from *Otō Monogatari*, the tale of (the battle of) Otō.[20] This clash occurred in 1400 when Ogasawara Nagahide's rearguard was cut off in the abandoned fort of Otō. After 20 days without food the desperate men decided to commit suicide or die fighting. The slaughter was considerable:

> Father and two sons, on the point of suicide, joined hands and faced west. In loud voices they earnestly chanted the *nembutsu*, the promise and the prayer [of Amida] to receive them and not to abandon them. And each, with repeated blows, committed suicide... Now, the next day, the eighteenth day of the tenth month, in the hour of the tiger [3:00–5:00 am] the forces of the vanguard attacked. They raced each other around and around the fort, took the heads of the dead, and dispatched the dying with a blade through the throat. They stopped those fleeing and cut off their arms and legs. They pursued the dying to the scattered places they had crawled to and took their heads. Their actions were indescribable. Now, the lay priest Kōsaka Munetsugu, second in command of the horse of the left, shut his eyes for a time. What he thought in his very heart was that this was nothing more than the Six Realms.[21]

The expression 'the Six Realms' refers to the Buddhist belief that there are six stages of existence between hell and heaven. All involve some degree of suffering, and in the age of *mappō* it was possible to experience the suffering of all of them here on earth.[22] The author of *Otō Monogatari* seems to see the battlefield as being equivalent to the lower realms of hungry ghosts and beasts, where men were degraded so much that they would even eat the raw flesh of their horses.[23] The only hope of escape from this awful world is the vow of Amida Buddha to rescue all sentient beings. Fortunately for the defenders of Otō, a community of *jishū* located nearby in the Zenkōji temple (in modern Nagano) came to the fort to do what they could to help and to assure them on this point:

> Now, the Tsumado *jishū* of Zenkoji and similarly the holy men of Junenji heard that the men at Otō had committed suicide. They hurried there and inspected the miserable state of the battlefield. It was a sight too awful to look upon. Men who only recently had appeared so fine and grand all lay dead upon the moor. The corpses of men lay strewn together with the carcasses of horses. [A carpet of] blood-stained creepers, fluttering in the wind like the red leaves of [Mount] Kōya, resembled red brocade spread out in the sun.
>
> Monks and priests who were relatives collected the remains and embraced the dead bodies. They grieved and wept without limit. Such a thing has never been heard of in the past nor seen in our own time. Those *jishū* gathered up one by one the corpses lying scattered here and there. Some they burnt and others they buried. They set up stupas and on each they bestowed *nembutsu*. Everywhere they raised the hope that Amida would come to lead them to paradise. More and more they acted with the mercy of Buddha. They went as far as to collect [the last] writings from the dead as souvenirs which were sent to the widows and orphans.[24]

A similar lament for the horror of the battlefield and the degraded state of humans who fight there comes from the eloquent and often angry brush of the monk Keinen, a Jōdo Shinshū priest from Usuki in Bungo province, who was taken along as a chaplain by Ota Kazuyoshi during Hideyoshi's second invasion of Korea in 1597. Like the author of *Otō Monogatari*, Keinen's diary likens the battlefield to the realm of beasts where the samurai lose every trace of human compassion. On one occasion the peasant labourers are beaten so severely that Keinen sees them metaphorically as so many 'dumb oxen', which are 'slaughtered, their hides are flayed and they are eaten'; this is the Realm of Beasts. On another occasion he makes his most despairing statement of all: 'I am fearful of all these things. Hell cannot be in any other place except here.' War had made men descend to the lowest of all the Six Worlds.[25]

One further element that added to the horror of the samurai battlefield was the well-known practice of cutting off and collecting the heads of dead enemies. The main focus came after a battle, when most of the ritual surrounding a

The horror of the battlefield is powerfully conveyed by this print of Akechi Mitsuchika at the battle of Yamazaki in 1582. During Hideyoshi's inspection of the battlefield the following day, Mitsuchika rose up from among a mound of corpses to try to kill him.

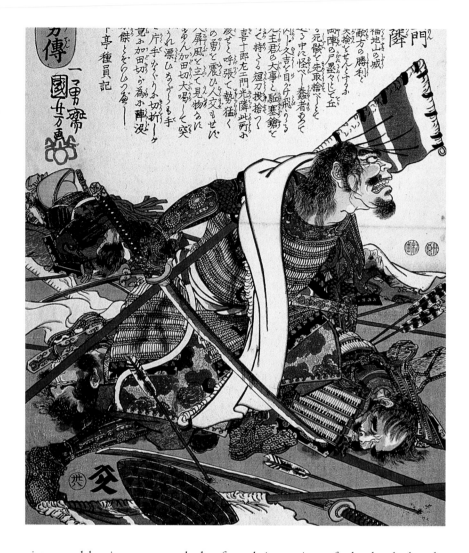

victory celebration concerned the formal inspection of the heads by the victorious general. He would sit in state, while one by one the heads were brought before him for comment. These ceremonies appear to have been quite informal affairs until the 14th century. The *Mōko Shūrai Ekotoba* shows a head inspection taking place during the Mongol invasions. The heads, from which blood is still seeping, have been casually placed on the ground.[26] The ceremony later grew into one of considerable formality to which the victorious commander would give his full attention – a matter that proved to be the undoing of Imagawa Yoshimoto in 1560, who was so engrossed in head-viewing that he suffered a surprise attack. A few hours later it was his own head that was being viewed by someone else.

The press of battle often left little opportunity for anything other than simple head identification; the formalities had to wait until later. During the

Age of Warring States it became most undesirable for a *daimyō* to be presented with an untidy trophy. Prior to his inspection the heads would be washed, the hair combed, and the resulting trophy made presentable by cosmetics, tasks traditionally done by women. The heads would then be mounted on a spiked wooden board with red labels for identification. This act of cleaning the heads was in part a sign of respect for fallen warriors. It also represented a tribute to the victors' pride as men who could defeat heroic enemies. The *Azuma Kagami* tells us how Minamoto Yoritomo exhibited the heads of 19 enemy samurai after the battle of Azukashiyama in 1189, while a 13th-century warrior called Obusuma Saburō liked to maintain a steady supply of fresh heads hanging on the fence surrounding the riding field of his home.[27]

A samurai general examines an enemy head brought before him.

When viewed purely as a means of proving one's merit, head collection would appear to have no religious context. However, although accounts of head-taking as proof of duty done dominate the narratives, there is also evidence that some heads were used as offerings to the *kami* in celebration of victory. On one occasion Minamoto Yoritomo went far beyond head collection and sacrificed a prisoner as part of his celebration of victory in his northern campaign. Elsewhere his brother Yoshitsune cut the heads off 20 men and offered them to the gods of war.[28]

The alternative to displaying heads as trophies was to return them to the victims' families after the inspection ceremony. This was a merciful act that went beyond mere generosity to a defeated enemy because of one little-known religious belief of the time. There was a deeply held feeling that a fragment of the deceased's mind and spirit could be found in every part of his body. If some parts were missing the spirit became unhappy in the next world.[29] For a dead samurai to have had his head removed would cause great problems both for him and his family. Samurai begged to have the heads of their dead comrades returned to them so that they were ensured rebirth in the life to come,[30] as in this *Taiheiki* account of the siege of Akasaka:

> Now there was a holy man who followed Homma to that place, and for his sake recited the name of Amida Buddha ten times at the last. This monk begged Homma's head to take back to Tennōji, where he spoke of all that had passed to Homma's son, Gennai Hyōe Suketada.[31]

In 1581 two senior retainers were sent to investigate what had happened at Shikano castle and discovered that a massacre had taken place. One thing that they did before returning was to match up and replace together the heads that had been separated from bodies.[32] One imagines that orders sometimes given by commanders during heated battles that heads should be 'cut and tossed' so as not to hinder the momentum of the fight[33], would have caused much distress.

In this terrible Realm of the Beasts that was the samurai battlefield the need to pacify the *goryō shinkō* of those who died there was acutely felt by the contemporary mind.[34] It was an impulse that went far beyond any human need to bury a corpse and remember a loved one. There was also considerable fear, because the vengeful spirits of the dead could cause havoc among the living by various sorts of natural disasters and pestilences. The belief that all spirits at death had 'sharp edges' was multiplied tenfold for an angry ghost produced in the horror of the battlefield.

From about the time of the 12th-century Gempei War, the initiative for commissioning memorial services for the dead of battles usually lay with either the reigning or the retired emperor.[35] The larger-than-life Minamoto Yoritomo provides an early exception to this rule by his founding of a temple in Kamakura to offer

OPPOSITE

For a dead samurai, having had his head removed would cause great problems both for him and his family. Heads thrown away, as in this print, would have caused much distress. The samurai pictured is Endō Naotsugu, who tried to kill Oda Nobunaga during the battle of Anegawa in 1570. He approached Nobunaga in the guise of a friendly warrior presenting him with a severed head, and when his true purpose was discovered he threw the head in the direction of his intended victim and died fighting.

prayers for the spirits of his brother Yoshitsune and the other samurai who had been killed in the northern campaign of 1189,[36] but the first samurai general to take on board wholeheartedly the duty of memorializing the dead was Ashikaga Takauji. As an earlier chapter showed, Takauji was a deeply religious man in a deeply religious age, and he began offering memorial services to pacify the 'evil spirits' of his Hōjō enemies in 1335. Two years later, at the behest of the Zen master Musō Soseki, he and his brother Tadayoshi began a remarkable religious building project, whereby a 'temple of peace in the realm' (*ankokuji*) and a 'pagoda of the Buddha's favour' (*rishōto*) were successfully built in each province. The *ankokuji*, all of which were Zen temples, were founded to provide a focus and a sacred space for the pacification of the restless spirits of the dead who had been killed in battle.[37]

In this way, for example, the massacred defenders of Kanegasaki castle, who were believed to have become *onryō*, might be placated.[38] These spirits were anonymous, but others were known by name. Emperor Sutoku and Fujiwara Yorinage, defeated and killed during the Hōgen Incident of 1156, became angry spirits. One very prominent *goryō shinkō* was the spirit of Taira Masakado, who was killed in battle in 940 and is enshrined in the Kanda Myōjin shrine in Tokyo.[39] Masakado was first worshipped there in 1309 after a series of floods, droughts and epidemics had been blamed on his unruly spirit. In the *Shōmonki*, the chronicle of Masakado's rebellion, his departed spirit sends a message back to earth to describe how he is suffering the torments of hell, where, 'My body was placed in the forest of sword-leaf trees where I was made to suffer, and my liver was roasted over smouldering embers in an iron cage... My brothers, you must fulfil my vow in order that I may escape from this suffering.'[40]

The shrine to Shōni Suketoki, a hero of the Mongol invasions, on the island of Iki.

There is an interesting modern coda to this story. Masakado had been a rebel against imperial rule, and in 1874, when the institution of the emperor was being strengthened against the memory of the overthrown Shogun, Masakado was condemned as an enemy of the emperor. As Emperor Meiji was planning to visit the Kanda Myōjin shrine, it was decided to move Masakado's spirit from the main shrine to a sub-shrine. But when this was done local people refused to go to the main shrine, boycotted its annual festival and held back on financial contributions. The reason they gave was that it was wise to keep an unruly spirit pacified, and that if Masakado's spirit was deprived of its proper shrine then it would start causing trouble again. He was eventually restored to his status as principal *kami* of the shrine in May 1984.[41]

Jizō is the protector of children, and this is the role symbolized by these childlike Jizō statues erected to commemorate *mizuko* (dead children). The emphasis is on providing a memorial for children who died very young, and also through stillbirths, miscarriages and abortion.

As the reader will no doubt have realized, customs regarding death provide a further example of the accommodative tendency in Japanese religion. Burying the dead and enshrining them are two separate but related activities that reflect, as it were, the 'division of labour' between Buddhism and Shintō. So, for example, the loyal Forty-Seven Rōnin are buried in Tokyo, where they performed their act of revenge, but since 1912 have been enshrined hundreds of miles away in Banshū Ako, their late lord's castle town; prayers may be offered to them in both places. Buddhism provided the essential ritualized link between the graveyard, the temple and the family *butsudan* with its gleaming black and gold *ihai*. As noted above, many would say it is too involved in these rituals and has become a vulgarized 'state religion' of 'funerary Buddhism', with a consequent loss of spirituality.[42] Shintō is involved more with rituals relating to birth and rites of passage, and is more communally orientated. Shintō shrines, where unhappy spirits such as Taira Masakado are enshrined for their own good and the good of the entire nation, are places where no body is buried, and are therefore very different in character from cemeteries. These points are of vital importance in considering the nature and function of Japan's most controversial shrine: the Yasukuni Jinja, built to enshrine the Japanese dead of her modern wars.

PACIFICATION AND PROTEST

Tokyo's Yasukuni shrine does not enshrine ancient *kami*, nor members of the imperial family, nor even exalted figures from Japanese history, but, in the main, individual commoners who died in the wars.[43] From the time of its founding the Yasukuni shrine received a respect exceeded only by the Great Shrine of Ise, a status it acquired when the emperor himself went there to pay tribute to the souls of the war dead. It was therefore a great honour to be enshrined there, but the political ideas that lay behind this simple act of religious charity are quite evident. As noted earlier, the need to inculcate the ordinary soldier with the spirit of the samurai provided an enormous challenge to the Meiji government. To the provision of patriotic Buddhist chaplains during this life the authorities added some reassurance of recognition in the afterlife. The act of enshrinement of a person at Yasukuni meant that he or she was symbolically changed from being a mere ancestor of some household to being attached to the nation as a whole.

Originally founded in Kyōto as the Shōkonsha ('the shrine for calling the spirits of the dead') the shrine was transferred to Tokyo in June 1879 and renamed the Yasukuni-jinja. The spirits of all those who had died in the fighting leading up to the Meiji Restoration were then transferred to Yasukuni from their previous places of enshrinement. Yasukuni means 'the shrine of the peaceful land', and from then on the spirits of soldiers killed in all the wars of Japan were enshrined there.[44] This now includes no fewer than 2,460,000 named individuals who died in battle or of disease or accidents while on active service. Some civilians who were mobilized by the military are also included, but not purely civilian non-combatants, such as the thousands who died in the fire-bombing of Tokyo. Nor are the spirits of those who died opposing the Meiji emperor included – they have a small memorial elsewhere that was erected in 1872. Because of the distinction between a shrine and a cemetery, all the Japanese war dead are buried somewhere else as well as being enshrined at Yasukuni. Curiously, Japan also has a Tomb of the Unknown Soldier, established in 1959, that houses the ashes of one person chosen to represent all the war dead.[45] Ninety-five per cent of the names in Yasukuni are of people who died between 1931 and 1945, so it is easy to see why the shrine has such an important role to play in the nation's remembrance.[46] Soldiers going off to war would often say to each other, with perhaps not a little touch of irony, 'See you in Yasukuni!'[47]

Until 1895 only those who actually died in battle were enshrined there. To die of wounds was regarded as a disgrace, though as the following example shows, there were exceptions. A soldier called Kuga Noboru was thought to have died fighting in China in 1931 and was scheduled to be enshrined at Yasukuni. However, he had in fact been captured and imprisoned. When he recovered sufficiently from his wounds he escaped from capture, reached the

The main hall of the Yasukuni shrine in Tokyo, founded to enshrine the spirits of the war dead. Note the large imperial chrysanthemum on the curtains.

Japanese lines and then committed suicide to atone for the disgrace of being taken alive. The shame he felt at his failure to die in action was echoed at an official level because he was removed from the list of those destined for the great privilege of being enshrined at Yasukuni. He was, however, reinstated after public opinion forced a special dispensation.[48]

During the Meiji Period the existence of Yasukuni provided a focus for the education of the nation's children about how they were expected to behave in similar circumstances:

> Around 1893 a board game became highly popular with school-children, in which the quickest way to win was to land on a certain square by a role of the dice. 'Death' in that position took the player to instant enshrinement at Yasukuni. The game, reinforced by the custom of school trips to Yasukuni, carried a powerful message. The notion that death in battle followed by enshrinement at Yasukuni was in fact a victory was voiced even by bereaved survivors.[49]

The most controversial aspect of the Yasukuni shrine is the inclusion among its millions of enshrined spirits of certain Class A war criminals who were executed after the Tokyo War Crimes Trials, such as the wartime Prime Minister Hideki Tōjō.[50] The 'child's guide' to Yasukuni describes them as follows: 'There are also 1,068 who had their lives cruelly taken after the war when they were falsely and one-sidedly branded as "war criminals" by the kangaroo court of the Allies who fought Japan.'[51]

These war criminals were not enshrined immediately after their executions but over 30 years later in a quiet ceremony in 1978. Few people were aware that this had happened until the Chinese government protested about the 1985 visit to Yasukuni by the then Japanese prime minister.[52] The year 1978 is significant because it was 33 years after the men's deaths, by which time the mourning process had finished and their spirits had become *kami*. To add to the controversy over their enshrinement, there has been a great deal of comment both within Japan and outside it over the visits to Yasukuni made by successive Japanese prime ministers since this date. Reported in the Western media as acts of 'worshipping the war dead' or 'condoning Japan's past aggression', these visits have provoked considerable protest in China and Korea. The first visit to cause controversy was made by the then Prime Minister Nakasone on the 40th anniversary of the end of World War II. Strangely enough, this was not the first visit by a prime minister. Official visits had been made as far back as 1951 with no major political repercussions, but Tōjō and the others were not enshrined at Yasukuni then.

Should the visits really be seen in this wholly negative light? As Kuroda reminds us, because Yasukuni enshrines people and not ancient *kami* the activities associated with such spirits of the dead fit in with beliefs about the

A detail from the graveyard of a Jōdō Shinshū temple in Takefu.

need to pacify angry spirits.[53] The name Yasukuni is also written with exactly the same characters that can also be read *ankoku*: the name given to the temples founded by Ashikaga Takauji in the 14th century to pacify the spirits of those killed in battle.

It is, however, important to realize that the notion of pacifying angry spirits at Yasukuni was not mentioned in the words used by the Meiji emperor at its dedication. Instead he stated that the spirits of the dead would be 'worshipped and admired'.[54] The pacification of angry ghosts only becomes apparent as an overt aim in 1969 in a government bill introduced to achieve control over the shrine by denying its religious nature, where it is stated that the shrine will 'pacify and appease' the spirits.[55] Nine years later the Class A war criminals were enshrined there, and from this time on Yasukuni became more than a shrine for honouring the dead who had fought to protect Japan from its enemies. The shrine now also had the role of protecting the country from certain spirits by ensuring their pacification. However, this is still a matter of controversy and some will argue that the spirits in Yasukuni are concerned solely with safeguarding the nation's peace and security.[56] Nevertheless, helped considerably by its chilling museum next door where Japan's recent military past is unexpectedly glorified in recently refurbished displays, Yasukuni still retains a role as a place where there is something quite sinister about the link between the samurai and the sacred.[57]

芳年武者无類

左兵衛佐源頼朝

EPILOGUE

It would be completely wrong to leave the reader with the impression that the image of the samurai and the sacred in modern Japan is manifested only through violence. The examples cited earlier of the Red Brigade and Aum Shinrikyō are aberrations, where the link between the samurai and the sacred has been seized upon and misused for political ends. The development of the martial arts as training for the mind and for the body, the appreciation of Japanese culture through Zen and other artistic expression, is the sacred legacy to which we must cling.

As noted earlier, the visitor to Japan today finds much that is religious, and most of it delights both the mind and the senses. Japanese religion, in its overt expression, is both welcoming and patient to the outsider. The discovery of a local shrine festival often turns out to be the highlight of any tourist's visit.[1] Dig a little more deeply and it is possible to observe respectfully and meaningfully a profound depth of religious expression. A walk through remote wooded mountains may reveal *yamabushi* (mountain ascetics) performing their pilgrimages in a classic instance of religious syncretism. Clad in white, they make an arduous journey that includes visits to mountain-top Buddhist temples, prayers at wayside Shintō shrines and folk-religious rituals along the way, in a journey that takes them symbolically through the Womb and Diamond mandalas of Shingon.[2]

As well as surviving and prospering, the world of the sacred in Japan has always been prepared to change. No more striking illustration of this phenomenon exists than the introduction into the rituals of long-established Shintō shrines of something that conveys a more modern message. The Kanamara shrine in Kawasaki is one of only a handful of Shintō shrines left in Japan where the focus of attention is on the human procreative act, the fertility

OPPOSITE

Mounted combat between two samurai.

A *yamabushi* pilgrim taking part in the pilgrimage from Yoshino to Kumano.

of which is expressed through unusual artefacts within the shrines, such as enormous wooden phalli.[3] The festival rituals associated with these objects are well known, well attended and largely misunderstood. The Kanamara shrine has gone one step further in its dealings with matters of human sexuality, and the unequivocal representation of the male sexual organ is now used also to convey the message of safer sex. Participants in the annual *matsuri* leave with *ofuda*, the little religious mementoes supplied on such occasions, which contain condoms as well as prayer slips. Even more striking is the new message introduced to the

Kabasan Tabako-jinja. As the name implies, the shrine exists because of the local speciality crop grown there:

> The area at the foot of the mountain is a production area for the whole country of celebrated leaf tobacco. Hail and thunder are tobacco's greatest enemies. To ward off these calamities, and to ensure bumper crops, prayers are offered every day to the guardian *kami* in Japan's unique tobacco shrine.[4]

The annual festival of the shrine involves a parade carrying a gigantic tobacco pipe, but whereas the Kanamara shrine has introduced an element that is complementary to its central message of fertility, the Kabasan shrine now invites people to come and pray for success in giving up smoking.

The world of the sacred in Japan is therefore one that is continually reinventing itself, and is a predominantly generous world into which even foreign and apparently competitive influences can be incorporated peacefully. But just as the discussion of the mind-set of the common soldier illustrated, when the sacred meets the samurai the perception of the one may not always meet the expectations of the other. So perhaps the last word should go to the character of the sceptical samurai, a figure created for the popular didactic

A Buddhist priest inside the main hall of his temple.

The Oniyo (devil's night) festival at Kurume, one of Japan's most spectacular New Year celebrations.

work *The Bag of Information for Citizens*, published in 1742. It is light fiction, but nothing shows better the wide range of attitudes and emotions that could sometimes be encountered:

> There is a story about a samurai who was dying, and to whose bed a monk came and said, 'You have done good service in this life, and so without question you will go to Paradise, so set your mind at ease.' 'And what kind of place is Paradise?' asked the samurai. 'It is a land where there is neither heat nor cold, and where food and drink can be got for the asking, a place of nothing but comfort and happiness.' 'Hmm,' replied the samurai, 'that kind of place is very suitable for court nobles, ladies in waiting, women, children and invalids, but I was born in a warrior family accustomed to brave the rain and the cold and to sleep on the ground with my head on a stone. Thus I have lived all my days so that I could render loyal service to my lord and destroy his enemies, and now I have come to die do you think I can change my nature? A beastly sort of place I consider your Paradise.'[5]

ENDNOTES

INTRODUCTION

1   From *Matsuura Hōin Seiken Nikki* in Kuwada et al. (eds), *Chōsen no eki (Nihon no Senshi*, Vol.5), Tokyo (1965) p.252.

2   Kuroda, Toshio, 'The Discourse on the "Land of the Kami" (shinkoku) in Medieval Japan: National Consciousness and International Awareness', *Japanese Journal of Religious Studies*, 23 (1996) pp.353–385.

3   Hori, Ichiro et al., *Japanese Religion: A Survey by the Agency for Cultural Affairs*, Tokyo (1972) p.12.

4   For two different interpretations of the Jingū myth see Arima, Toshio, 'The Myth of the Goddess of the Undersea World and the Tale of Empress Jingū's Subjugation of Silla', *Japanese Journal of Religious Studies*, 20 (1993) pp.95–185; and Allen, Chizuko, 'Empress Jingū: a Shamaness Ruler in Early Japan', *Japan Forum*, 15 (2003) pp.81–98.

5   A bodhissatva is dedicated to assisting all sentient beings achieve complete Buddhahood.

THE WAY OF THE GODS

1   For fascinating accounts of what actually happens during shrine visits, see Nelson, John K., 'Freedom of Expression: The Very Modern Practice of Visiting a Shinto Shrine', *Japanese Journal of Religious Studies*, 23 (1996) pp.117–153; reprinted in Nelson, John K., *Enduring Identities: The Guise of Shinto in Contemporary Japan*, Honolulu (2000) pp.22–52; and Reader, Ian, *Religion in Contemporary Japan*, London (1991) especially pp.134–167.

2   This perceived 'Japanese-ness' of Shintō may be illustrated in a different and less positive way. When Japan's colonial role over Korea ended in 1945 the 1,133 Shintō shrines erected in Korea were speedily destroyed by the local population, who had always seen them as a symbol of occupation. See Grayson, James H., 'Shinto and Japanese Popular Religion: Case Studies of Multi-variant Practice from Kyushu and Okinawa', *Japan Forum*, 17 (2005) p.364.

3   Most of the others are shrines to Inari, the *kami* of rice, and are affiliated to the Fushimi Inari shrine near Kyōto.

4   Ueda, Kenji, *Shinto*, Tokyo, no date given, p.2.

5   Motoori Norinaga's *Kojiden* quoted in Matsumae, Takeshi, 'Early Kami Worship' in Brown, Delmer M. (ed.), *The Cambridge History of Japan Volume 1, Ancient Japan*, Cambridge (1993) p.318.

6   Kishimoto, Hideo, 'The Worship of Mt. Miwa', in *Omiwa Shrine* (an English-language booklet produced by the Omiwa Jinja), Sakurai, not

dated, p. 7. Mount Sinai, by contrast, which is important to three religions, is open to pilgrims and tourists alike. Nevertheless the ancient monastery of St Catherine, which lies at its foot, was given special protection by the Prophet Muhammad, a gesture that any Japanese would fully understand.

7   Hidemoto, Okochi, *Chōsen ki* in *Zoku Gunsho Ruijū*, Tokyo (1933) p.281.

8   Shillony, Ben-Ami, *Enigma of the Emperors: Sacred Subservience in Japanese History*, Folkestone (2005) p.4.

9   Matsumae, 'Early Kami Worship', p.324. See also Breen, John and Teeuwen, Mark, *Shinto in History: Ways of the Kami*, Richmond (2000) pp.1–3.

10   Tsunoda, R. et al., *Sources of Japanese Tradition*, Vol. 1, New York (1964) p.30.

11   For examples see Matsumae, 'Early Kami Worship' pp.338–347.

12   Grayson, James H., 'Susa-no-o: a Culture Hero from Korea', *Japan Forum*, 14 (2002) pp.465–487.

13   Reader, Ian et al., *Japanese Religions Past and Present*, Folkestone (1993) p.169.

14   Teeuwen, Mark and Scheid, Bernhard, 'Tracing Shinto in the History of Kami Worship', *Japanese Journal of Religious Studies*, 29 (2000) p.195.

15   Kuroda, Toshio, 'Shinto in the History of Japanese Religion', *Journal of Japanese Studies*, 7 (1981) pp.1–21; reprinted with commentary in Tanabe, George (ed.), *Religions of Japan in Practice*, Princeton (1999) pp.451–467.

16   McMullin, Neil, 'Historical and Historiographical Issues in the Study of Pre-Modern Japanese Religions', *Japanese Journal of Religious Studies*, 16 (1989) p.5.

17   McMullin, 'Historical and Historiographical Issues', p.6.

18   Breen, *Shinto in History*, p.3.

19   For 'traditional' studies of Shintō see Harada, Tasuku, *The Faith of Japan*, New York (1926); Herbert, Jean, *Shintō: At the Fountainhead of Japan*, London (1967); Ono, Sokyō, *Shintō: The Kami Way*, Rutland (1962).

20   Kasahara, Kazuo (ed.), *A History of Japanese Religion*, Tokyo (2001) pp.27–28; Yamagata, Mariko, 'The Shakadō Figurines and Middle Jōmon Ritual in the Kofu Basin', *Japanese Journal of Religious Studies*, 19 (1992) pp.129–138.

21   Matsumae, 'Early Kami Worship', p.330.

22   Matsumae, 'Early Kami Worship', p.331.

23   Hudson, Mark J., 'Rice, Bronze and Chieftains – An Archaeology of Yayoi Ritual', *Japanese Journal of Religious Studies*, 19 (1992) pp.139–189.

24   Tsunoda, *Sources*, p. 6.

25   Kasahara, *A History*, p.37.

26   Herbert, *Shintō*, p. 92.

27   Matsumae, 'Early Kami Worship', p.332.

28   Kasahara, *A History*, pp.38–45; Ishino, Hironobu, 'Rites and Rituals of the Kofun Period', *Japanese Journal of Religious Studies*, 19 (1992) pp.191–216.

29   It is sometimes stated that the reasons why most imperial *kofun* have never been excavated is that the imperial family are afraid that this will expose their ancestors as Korean invaders rather than as descendants of *kami*. This is challenged in Edwards, Walter, 'Contested Access: The Imperial Tombs in the Postwar Period', *Journal of Japanese Studies*, 26 (2000) pp.371–392. The 'horse rider' theory, whereby the Jingū legend is completely reversed, is associated particularly with the Japanese scholar Egami Namio, and was made known to the West largely through Ledyard, Gary, 'Galloping Along with the Horseriders: Looking for the Founders of Japan', *The Journal of Japanese Studies*, 2 (1975) pp.217–254. For a refutation see Edwards, Walter, 'Event and Process in the Founding of Japan: The Horserider Theory in Archaeological Perspective', *Journal of Japanese* Studies, 9 (1983) pp.263–295. See also Arima, Toshio, 'The Myth of the Goddess', pp.95–185.

30   Nakakami, Hirochika, 'The "Separate" Coexistence of Kami and Hotoke – a look at Yorishiro', *Japanese Journal of Religious Studies*, 10 (1983) pp.65–86.

31   Grapard, Alan, 'Flying Mountains and Walkers of Emptiness: Towards a Definition of Sacred Space in Japanese Religions', *History of Religions*, 21 (1982) p.198.

32   Aston, W. G., *Shintō, or the Way of the Gods*, London (1905) p.26.

33   Czaja, Michael, *Gods of Myth and Stone: Phallicism in Japanese Folk Religion*, New York (1974) p.142.

BUDDHA AND THE BUSHI

1   For a controversial opinion of Prince Shōtoku see Yoshida, Kazuhiko, 'Revisioning Religion in Ancient Japan', *Japanese Journal of Religious Studies*, 30 (2003) p.4. A detailed discussion appears in Deal, William, 'Hagiography and History: The Image of Prince Shōtoku', in Tanabe, George (ed.), *Religions of Japan in Practice*, Princeton (1999) pp.316–333.

2   Yoshida, 'Revisioning Religion', p.5.

3   Tyler, Royall, *The Miracles of the Kasuga Deity*, New York (1990).

4   Chiyonobu, Yoshimasa, 'Recent Archaeological Excavations at the Tōdai-ji', *Japanese Journal of Religious Studies*, 19 (1992) pp.245–254.

5   Matsumae, 'Early Kami Worship', p.357.

6   Kasahara, *A History*, pp.141–143.

7   Kasahara, *A History*, p.144.

8   Tyler, Susan, 'Honji Suijaku Faith', *Japanese Journal of Religious Studies*, 16 (1989) p.229.

9   Paine, Robert and Soper, Alexander, *The Art and Architecture of Japan*, London (1955).

10   Yoshida, 'Revisioning Religion', p.18; Kasahara, *A History*, p.76.

11   Adolphson, Michael, 'Enryakuji – An Old Power in a New Era', in Mass, Jeffrey P., *The Origins of Japan's Medieval World: Courtiers, Clerics, Warriors and Peasants in the Fourteenth Century*, Stanford (1997) p.246.

12   Lai, Whalen, 'Why the Lotus Sutra? On the Historic Significance of Tendai', *Japanese Journal of Religious Studies*, 14 (1987) p.83.

13   Abe, Ryuichi, 'Saicho and Kukai: A Conflict of Interpretations', *Japanese Journal of Religious Studies*, 22 (1995) pp.103–137.

14   Hall, Manly P., *Koyasan: Sanctuary of Esoteric Buddhism*, Los Angeles (1970) p.9.

15   Rhodes, Robert F., 'The Kaihōgyō Practice of Mount Hiei', *Japanese Journal of Religious Studies*, 14 (1987) pp.185–202; Reader, *Religion*, pp.124–127.

16   Paine, *The Art*, pp.210ff.

17   Paine, *The Art*, pp.216–221.

18   Tyler, 'Honji Suijaku Faith', p.229.

19   Kasahara, *A History*, p.306; Antoni, Klaus, 'The "Separation of Gods and Buddhas" at Omiwa Jinja in Meiji Japan', *Japanese Journal of Religious Studies*, 22 (1995) p.144.

20   Kuroda, Toshio, 'The World of Spirit Pacification: Issues of State and Religion', *Japanese Journal of Religious Studies*, 23 (1996) p.342.

21   Hall, *Koyasan*, p.37.

22   Sadler, A. L., *The Maker of Modern Japan: The Life of Tokugawa Ieyasu*, London (1937) pp.180–181.

23   Kasahara, *A History*, p.126.

24   Marra, Michelle, 'The Development of Mappo Thought in Japan (I)', *Japanese Journal of Religious Studies*, 15 (1988) pp.25–54.

25   Marra, 'The Development', p.51.

26   Kasahara, *A History*, p.126.

27   Shively, Donald H. and McCullough, William (eds), *The Cambridge History of Japan Volume 2, Heian Japan*, Cambridge (1999) p.682.

28   McCullough, Helen, *The Tale of the Heike*, Stanford (1988) p.50.

29   Sadler, A. L., 'Heike Monogatari', *Transactions of the Asiatic Society of Japan*, 46 (1918) pp.48–52.

30   Moerman, David, 'The Ideology of Landscape and the Theatre of State: Insei Pilgrimage to Kumano (1090–1220)', *Japanese Journal of Religious Studies*, 24 (1997) p.352.

31 Shinoda, Minoru, *The Founding of the Kamakura Shogunate 1180–1185, with selective translations from the Azuma Kagami*, New York (1960) p.151. The Three Treasures are the Buddha, the Law and the Priesthood: the three precious elements that made up Buddhism.

32 Shively, *The Cambridge History*, p.706.

33 Shinoda, *The Founding*, p.204.

34 Shinoda, *The Founding*, p.205.

35 Moerman, 'The Ideology', p.353.

36 Sadler, 'Heike Monogatari', pp.257–258.

37 Sadler, 'Heike Monogatari', p.1.

THE GODS GO TO WAR

1 McCullough, Helen, *The Taiheiki: A Chronicle of Medieval Japan*, New York (1959) p.184.

2 Conlan, Thomas D., *State of War: The Violent Order of Fourteenth Century Japan*, Ann Arbor (2003) p.173.

3 Farris, Wayne W., *Heavenly Warriors: The Evolution of Japan's Military 500–1300*, Harvard (1992) p.25.

4 McCullough, *The Taiheiki*, p.252.

5 Conlan, *State of War*, p.175.

6 Sadler, 'Heike Monogatari', p.242.

7 Shinoda, *The Founding*, p.150.

8 Collcutt, Martin, 'Religion in the Life of Minamoto Yoritomo and the Early Kamakura Bakufu' in Kornicki, P. F. and McMullen, I. J. (eds.), *Religion in Japan: Arrows to Heaven and Earth*, Cambridge (1996) pp.94–95.

9 Shinoda, *The Founding*, p.157; Colcutt, 'Religion', p.95.

10 Conlan, *State of War*, p.174.

11 Shinoda, *The Founding*, p.163.

12 Collcutt, 'Religion', p.98.

13 Shinoda, *The Founding*, p.167.

14 Kannon, the Buddhist Goddess of Mercy, represents another borrowing from Indian religious tradition. Originally Avalokiteśvara, Kannon came to Japan and changed gender on the way. See Kasahara, *A History*, p.136.

15 Shinoda, *The Founding*, p.168.

16 Shinoda, *The Founding*, p.184.

17 Collcutt, 'Religion', p.109.

18 Shinoda, *The Founding*, pp.188–189.

19 Shinoda, *The Founding*, p.296.

20 Sadler, 'Heike Monogatari', p.251.

21 Ironically, the lost sacred sword was actually a sacred replica treated with as much reverence as the original. See Turnbull, Stephen, *Samurai: The World of the Warrior*, Oxford (2003) pp.29–45.

22 Varley, Paul, *Warriors of Japan as Portrayed in the War Tales*, Honolulu (1994) p.86.

23 Shinoda, *The Founding*, p.330. This is the probable origin of the *Heike Monogatari* story of Mongaku bringing Yoshitomo's skull to Yoritomo to goad him to rebellion. See above and Sadler, 'Heike Monogatari', p.242.

24 Fogel, Joshua A. (ed.), *Sagacious Monks and Bloodthirsty Warriors: Chinese Views of Japan in the Ming-Qing Period*, Norwalk, CT (2002) p.21.

25 Jansen, Marius B., *Warrior Rule in Japan*, Cambridge (1995) p.54.

26 Hori, Kyotsu, *The Mongol Invasions and the Kamakura Bakufu*, unpublished PhD thesis, Columbia University (1967) p.139.

27 Jansen, *Warrior Rule*, p.56.

28 Large sections are reproduced in Smith, Bradley, *Japan: A History in Art*, London (1972) pp.106–121.

29 These have been extensively studied by Thomas Conlan in his fascinating book *In Little Need of Divine Intervention: Takezaki Suenaga's Scrolls of the Mongol Invasions of Japan*, Cornell University (2001).

30 Hori, *The Mongol Invasions*, pp.173–176.

31 Hori, *The Mongol Invasions*, p.173.

32 Conlan, *State of War*, p.166.

33 Hori, *The Mongol Invasions*, p.174.

34 Hori, *The Mongol Invasions*, p.175.

35 Made accessible to an English-speaking audience through Katō Bunnō et al., *The Threefold Lotus Sutra*, New York (1975).

36 Tsunoda, *Sources*, p.214.

37 Kasahara, *A History*, p.258.

38 Sanson, George, *Japan: A Short Cultural History* (Revised Edition), New York (1943) p.334.

39 Sanson, *Japan*, p.333.

40 Stone, Jacqueline, 'Rebuking the Enemies of the *Lotus*: Nichirenist Exclusivism in Historical Perspective', *Japanese Journal of Religious Studies*, 21 (1994) pp.231–259.

41 Tsunoda, *Sources*, p.220.

42 McCullough, *The Taiheiki*, p.290.

43 Conlan, *State of War*, p.187.

44 Kasahara, *A History*, p.139.

45 Kitagawa, Joseph M., *Religion in Japanese History*, New York (1966) pp.82–85.

46 Harrison, Elizabeth G., 'Mizuko kuyō: the Re-production of the Dead in Contemporary Japan', in Kornicki and McMullen, *Religion in Japan*, pp.250–266; Lafleur, William R., 'Buddhism and Abortion: "The Way to Memorialize One's Mizuko"', in Tanabe, *Religions*, pp.193–196.

47   Kitagawa, *Religion*, p.84.

48   Conlan, *State of War*, p.188.

WARRIORS OF THE PURE LAND

1   Marra, 'The Development', p.48.

2   Kasahara, *A History*, pp.114–115.

3   Kasahara, *A History*, pp.170–171.

4   Kasahara, *A History*, pp.191–193.

5   Rogers, Minor L., 'Rennyo and Jōdo Shinshū Piety: The Yoshizaki
      Years', *Monumenta Nipponica*, 36 (1981) p.24.

6   Marra, Michelle, 'The Development of Mappo Thought (II)', p.298.
      For a brief but succinct summary of Shinran's teachings see Kasahara,
      A History, pp.193–195. See also Soga, Ryojin, 'The Core of Shinshū',
      Japanese Journal of Religious Studies, 11 (1984) pp.221–242.

7   Tsunoda, *Sources*, p.203.

8   Rogers, 'Rennyo', p.21.

9   Sugiyama, Shigeki, 'Honganji in the Muromachi-Sengoku Period:
      Taking up the Sword and Its Consequences', *Pacific World: Journal of the
      Institute of Buddhist Studies*, 10 (1994) p.64.

10   This is the concept of *kenmon* ('powerful lineages' or 'ruling elites').
      The idea was introduced by the scholar Kuroda Toshio. According to
      his approach, between the 11th and 15th centuries power in Japan was
      shared by a number of elite groups who were the leaders of three
      power blocs: the *kuge* (court nobles), the *buke* (the samurai warrior
      aristocracy) and the *jisha* (shrines and temples). Their common cause
      provided a unifying ideology for the state. The imperial law (*ōbō*) and
      Buddhist teachings (*buppō*) were like the two wheels of a cart. For
      a very clear exposition of Kuroda's theory see Dobbins, James C.,
      'Editor's Introduction: Kuroda Toshio and His Scholarship', *Japanese
      Journal of Religious Studies*, 23 (1996) pp.218–232, especially
      pp.219–225. The rest of Volume 23, parts 3–4, contains papers by
      Kuroda.

11   Adolphson, Michael, 'Enryakuji – An Old Power in a New Era', in
      Mass, Jeffrey P., *The Origins of Japan's Medieval World: Courtiers, Clerics,
      Warriors and Peasants in the Fourteenth Century*, Stanford (1997) p.238. See
      also Adolphson's more recent work *The Gates of Power: Monks, Courtiers
      and Warriors in Premodern Japan*, Honolulu (2000).

12   Tsunoda, *Sources*, p.205.

13   Sadler, *The Maker*, p.66.

14   From *Hoan Nobunaga-ki* as translated in Tsunoda, *Sources*, p.305.

15   Lamers, Jeroen, *Japonius Tyrannus: The Japanese Warlord Oda Nobunaga
      Reconsidered*, Leiden (2000) p.76.

16   Rhodes, 'The Kaihōgyō Practice of Mount Hiei', pp.185–202.

17   Elison, George, 'The Cross and the Sword: Patterns of Momoyama History', in Elison, George and Smith, Bardwell L. (eds.), *Warlords, Artists and Commoners: Japan in the Sixteenth Century*, Honolulu (1981) p.71.

18   Elison, 'The Cross', p.72.

19   Ota Gyuichi, *Shinchōkōki*, ed. by Kuwada, Tadachika, Tokyo (1965) p.180.

20   Lamers, *Japonius Tyrannus*, p. 170.

21   Saeki, Tetsuya, 'Ikkō-ikki saigo no kyoten Torigoe Futoge', in *Maeda Toshiie* (Rekishi Gunzo 'Sengoku Selection' Series), Tokyo (2002) pp.26–27.

22   Lu, David J. *Japan: A Documentary History*, Vol. 1, New York (1997) p.195.

ONWARD, CHRISTIAN SAMURAI!

1   The arrival of Europeans in Japan has been exhaustively treated in Lidin, Olof G., *Tanegashima – The Arrival of Europeans in Japan*, Copenhagen (2002).

2   Cast-iron Chinese hand guns with short barrels had been known in Japan since 1510. They were used in battle as late as 1548, but were rapidly supplanted by arquebuses of Japanese manufacture. These had been copied from the Portuguese originals introduced in 1543 and were probably first fired in anger against Chinese pirates in 1548. See Turnbull, Stephen, 'War Trade and Piracy: Military and Diplomatic Relations between China, Korea and Japan and Their Influence on Japanese Military Technology', *Royal Armouries Yearbook*, 2 (1997) p.152.

3   Boxer, Charles, *Jan Compagnie in War and Peace 1602–1799: A Short History of the Dutch East-India Company*, Hong Kong (1979) p.2.

4   Boxer, Charles, *The Christian Century in Japan 1549–1650*, Manchester (1951) p.37.

5   Massarella, Derek, *A World Elsewhere: Europe's Encounter with Japan in the Sixteenth and Seventeenth Centuries*, New Haven (1990) p.40.

6   Elisonas, Jurgis, 'Christianity and the Daimyo', in Hall, John Whitney and McClain, James (eds), *The Cambridge History of Japan Volume 4, Early Modern Japan*, Cambridge (1991) p.308.

7   Elisonas, 'Christianity', p.309.

8   Boxer, *The Christian Century*, pp.54–55.

9   Turnbull, Stephen, *Japanese Castles 1540–1640*, Oxford (2003) p.29.

10   Lamers, *Japonius Tyrannus*, p.77.

11   Elison, George, *Deus Destroyed: The Image of Christianity in Early Modern Japan*, Harvard (1973) Note 78, p.303.

12   Turnbull, Stephen, *The Samurai Sourcebook*, London (1998) p.305.

13   Elisonas, 'Christianity', p.339.

14   Cary, Otis, *A History of Christianity in Japan: Roman Catholic, Greek Orthodox and Protestant Missions*, Rutland (1976) p.59.

15   Elison, *Deus Destroyed*, p.89.

16   Conlan, *State of War*, p.192.

17   Murdoch, James, *A History of Japan*, Vol. II, London (1925) p.108.

18   Elison, *Deus Destroyed*, p.24.

19   Dautremer, J., 'The Vendetta or Legal Revenge in Japan', *Transactions of the Asiatic Society of Japan*, 13 (1885) pp.82–89.

20   From his *Nef des Princes de Batailles*, quoted in J. R. Hale's 'War and Public Opinion in Renaissance Italy', in Hale, J. R. (ed.), *Renaissance War Studies*, London (1983) p.401.

21   The story of Takayama Ukon and the Araki affair appears in Elison, *Deus Destroyed*, pp.49–51; and Lamers, *Japonius Tyrannus*, pp.174–179.

22   Elison, *Deus Destroyed*, p.114.

23   Elison, *Deus Destroyed*, p.110.

24   Elison, *Deus Destroyed*, p.118.

25   Turnbull, Stephen, *Samurai Invasion: Japan's Korean War 1592–1598*, London (2002).

26   Elisonas, Jurgis, 'The Inseparable Trinity: Japan's Relations with China and Korea' in Hall and McClain, *The Cambridge History of Japan Volume 4*, p.273.

27   Cory, Ralph M., 'Some Notes on Father Gregorio de Cespedes: Korea's First European Visitor', *Transactions of the Korean Branch of the Royal Asiatic Society*, 27 (1937) pp.1–45.

28   Cory, 'Some notes', p.12.

29   Cory, 'Some notes', p.42.

30   Cory, 'Some notes', p.43.

31   Cory, 'Some notes', p.14.

32   Cory, 'Some notes', p.14.

33   Cory, 'Some notes', p.44.

THE SAMURAI AND THE SECRET

1   Sadler, *The Maker*, p.190.

2   Thompson, E. M. (ed.), *Diary of Richard Cocks, Cape-merchant in the English Factory in Japan 1615–1622, with correspondence*, Hakluyt Society, 1st Series 66, London (1883) Vol. 2, p.240. For clarity I have modernized the spelling in this and all subsequent similar quotations.

3   Sadler, *The Maker*, p.189.

4   Boxer, Charles, 'Notes on Early European Military Influence in Japan (1543–1853)', *Transactions of the Asiatic Society of Japan*, 2nd Series, 8 (1931) p.73.

5   Sadler, *The Maker*, p.190.

6   Sadler, *The Maker*, p.190.

7   Wild, Anthony, *The East India Company: Trade and Conquest from 1600*, London (1999) p.11.

8   Wild, *The East India Company*, p.29.

9   Farrington, Anthony, *The English Factory in Japan 1613–1623*, Vol. 1, London (1991) p.1.

10   Farrington, *The English Factory*, p.72.

11   Farrington, *The English Factory*, p.209.

12   Thompson, *Diary of Richard Cocks*, Vol. 2, p.44.

13   Thompson, *Diary of Richard Cocks*, Vol. 2, p.294.

14   Thompson, *Diary of Richard Cocks*, Vol. 2, p.85.

15   Thompson, *Diary of Richard Cocks*, Vol. 2, p.294.

16   Turnbull, Stephen, *Osaka 1615: The Last Samurai Battle*, Oxford (2006).

17   Boxer, *The Christian Century*, p.327.

18   Ohashi, Yukihiro, 'New Perspectives on the Early Tokugawa Persecution', in Breen, John and Williams, Mark (eds), *Japan and Christianity: Impacts and Responses*, Basingstoke (1996) pp.46–62.

19   Farrington, *The English Factory*, p.554.

20   Boxer, *The Christian Century*, p.344.

21   Farrington, *The English Factory*, p.134.

22   Anesaki, Masaharu, 'Persecution of Kirishitan after the Shimabara Insurrection', *Monumenta Nipponica*, 1 (1938) p.295.

23   For accounts of Neo-Confucianism see Kitagawa, *Religion in Japanese History*, pp.149–176; Reischauer, Edwin O. and Fairbank, John K., *East Asia: The Great Tradition*, Boston (1958) pp.616–617 and 657–659.

24   Nosco, Peter, 'Keeping the Faith: Bakuhan Policy Towards Religions in Seventeenth-Century Japan', in Kornicki, *Religion in Japan*, pp.135–155.

25   Marcure, Kenneth, 'The Danka System', *Monumenta Nipponica*, 40 (1985) pp.39–67.

26   Kitagawa, *Religion*, p.164.

27   Elison, *Deus Destroyed*, p.204.

28   Boxer, *The Christian Century*, pp.352–353.

29   Cieslik, Hubert, 'The Case of Christovão Ferreira', *Monumenta Nipponica*, 29 (1973) pp.1–54.

30   Boxer, *The Christian Century*, p.361.

31   Turnbull, Stephen, *The Kakure Kirishitan of Japan: A Study of their Development, Beliefs and Rituals to the Present Day*, Folkestone (1998).

32   Turnbull, *Kakure Kirishitan*, pp.47–48.

33   Tagita, Kōya, *Showa Jidai no Senpuku Kirishitan*, Tokyo (1954) pp.267 and 343.

34   Kondō, Gizaemon, *Ikitsuki shi kō*, Sasebo (1977) p.57.

35   Morris, Ivan, *The Nobility of Failure: Tragic Heroes in the History of Japan*, London (1975) pp.143–179.

36   Murdoch, *History of Japan*, p.657.

37   Morris, *The Nobility of Failure*, p.167.

38   Murdoch, *History of Japan*, p.657.

39   Morris, *The Nobility of Failure*, p.167.

40   Toby, Ronald P., *State and Diplomacy in Early Modern Japan: Asia in the Development of the Tokugawa Bakufu*, Princeton (1984).

41   Doolan, P., 'The Dutch in Japan', *History Today* (April 2000) p.37.

42   Glamann, K., *Dutch-Asiatic Trade 1620–1740*, Copenhagen (1958) pp.57–58.

43   Boxer, 'Notes', p.72.

44   Boxer, 'Notes', p.87.

45   Wild, *The East India Company*, p.33.

46   Van Heiken, M., *The Catholic Church in Japan since 1859*, London (1963) p.12.

47   Marnas, J., *La Religion de Jésus, Iaso Ja-kyo ressuscitée au Japon dans la seconde moitiée du XIXe*, Siècle Paris (1896) p.488.

48   Turnbull, *The Kakure Kirishitan*, p.52.

49   Turnbull, *The Kakure Kirishitan*, p.187.

50   Gentilcore, David, *From Bishop to Witch: The System of the Sacred in Early Modern Terra d'Otranto*, Manchester (1993) p.100.

51   Duffy, Eamon, *The Stripping of the Altars: Traditional Religion in England, 1400–1580*, Yale (1993) p.282.

52   Turnbull, *The Kakure Kirishitan*, p.190.

ZEN AND THE SAMURAI

1   An excellent and easily understood introduction to Zen Buddhism in Japan may be found in Tsunoda, *Sources*, p.226ff.

2   Joly, H. L., *Legend in Japanese Art*, London (1908) p.52.

3   Tsunoda, *Sources*, p.233.

4   Tsunoda, *Sources*, p.234.

5   Suzuki, D. T., *Zen and Japanese Culture*, Princeton (1970) p.20.

6   Suzuki, D. T., *The Awakening of Zen*, London (1987) p.57.

7   Collcut, Martin, 'The Zen Monastery in Kamakura Society', in Mass, Jeffrey P. (ed.), *Court and Bakufu in Japan: Essays in Kamakura History*, Stanford (1982) p.193.

8   Nukariya, Kaiten, *The Religion of the Samurai*, London (1913) pp.35–39.

9   Varley, H. Paul, 'Ashikaga Yoshimitsu and the World of Kitayama: Social Change and Shogunal Patronage in Early Muromachi Japan', in Hall, John Whitney and Toyoda, Takeshi (eds), *Japan in the Muromachi Age*, Berkeley (1977) p.202.

10   Engel, D. H., *Japanese Gardens for Today*, Tokyo (1959) p.21.

11   Tsunoda, *Sources*, p.280.

12   Tyler, Royall, 'Buddhism in Noh', *Japanese Journal of Religious Studies*, 14 (1987) pp.19–52.

13   Sadler, A. L., *Cha-no-yu the Japanese Tea Ceremony*, Rutland (1962) p.168.

14   Sadler, *Cha-no-yu*, p.167.

15   Sadler, *Cha-no-yu*, p.169.

16   Quoted in Engel, *Japanese Gardens*, p.13.

17   Friday, Karl F., *Legacies of the Sword: The Kashima Shinryū and Samurai Martial Culture*, Honolulu (1997).

18   Fukushima, *Bushido*, p.85.

19   Reader, Ian, 'Pilgrimage as Cult: The Shikoku Pilgrimage as a Window on Japanese Religion' in Kornicki and McMullen, *Religion in Japan*, pp.267–286.

20   Friday, *Legacies*, p.161.

21   Friday, *Legacies*, pp.8 and 163.

22   Sollier, A., *Japanese Archery: Zen in Action*, Tokyo (1969) p.23.

23   Herrigel, Eugen, *Zen in the Art of Archery*, trans. from the German by R. F. C. Hull, London (1953).

24   Yamada, Shoji, 'The Myth of Zen in the Art of Archery', *Japanese Journal of Religious Studies*, 28 (2001) pp.1–30.

25   Yamada, Shoji, 'The Myth of Zen', p.27.

THE WAYS OF THE WARRIOR

1   Nitobe, Inazo, *Bushido: The Soul of Japan*, New York (1905).

2   Shimazu, Naoko, 'The Myth of the "Patriotic Soldier": Japanese attitudes Towards Death in the Russo-Japanese War', *War and Society* (2001) p.69.

3   Hurst, G. Cameron, 'Death, Honor and Loyalty: The Bushido Ideal', *Philosophy East and West*, 40 (1990) pp.511–527.

4   Nitobe, *Bushido*, p.11.

5   Tsunoda, *Sources*, p.165.

6   Tsunoda, *Sources*, pp.284–285.

7   Wilson, William Scott, *Ideals of the Samurai: Writings of Japanese Warriors*, Los Angeles (1982) pp.121–122.

8   Ooms, Herbert, *Tokugawa Ideology: Early Constructs, 1570–1680*, Princeton (1985) pp.66–69.

9   Fukushima, Shoichi, *Bushido in Tokugawa Japan: A Reassessment of the Warrior Ethos*, unpublished PhD thesis, Berkeley (1984) pp.80–81.

10   Kitagawa, *Religion*, p.153.

11   Fukushima, *Bushido*, p.56.

12   Tsunoda, *Sources*, p.346.

13   Fukushima, *Bushido*, p.56.

14   Tsunoda, *Sources*, p.346.

15   Mitford, A. B. (Lord Redesdale), *Tales of Old Japan* (Reprinted), Rutland (1966) p.39.

16   McMullen, James, 'Confucian Perspectives on the Ako Revenge: Law and Moral Agency', *Monumenta Nipponica*, 58 (2003) pp.293–315.

17   Dautremer, 'The Vendetta', p.86.

18   Bitō, Masahide, 'The Akō Incident (1701–1703)', *Monumenta Nipponica*, 58 (2003) pp.149–169; Smith, Henry D. II, 'The Capacity of Chūshingura', *Monumenta Nipponica*, 58 (2003) pp.1–37.

19   Yamamoto, Tsunetomo, *The Book of the Samurai: Hagakure*, trans. by William Scott Wilson, Tokyo (1979) p.29.

20   McMullen, 'Confucian Perspectives', p.310.

21   Tucker, John Allen, 'Rethinking the Ako Ronin Debate: The Religious Significance of Chūshin Gishi', *Japanese Journal of Religious Studies*, 26 (1999) pp.1–37

22   Tucker, 'Rethinking', p.29.

23   Chamberlain, Basil Hall, *The Invention of a New Religion*, London (1912).

24   Kitagawa, *Religion*, p.186.

25   Shimazu, 'The Myth', p.73.

26   Yamamoto, *Hagakure*, p.164.

27   Shimazu, 'The Myth', p.87.

28   Shimazu, 'The Myth', p.87.

29   Shimazu, 'The Myth', p.79.

30   Von Durkheim, Karlfried, *The Japanese Cult of Tranquillity*, London (1974) p.44.

31   Yamamoto, *Hagakure*, p.17.

32   Morris, *The Nobility*, p.320.

33   Allen, Louis, 'Death and Honour in Japan', *The Listener* (24 June 1967) pp.1–4.

34   Reader, Ian, *Religious Violence in Contemporary Japan: The Case of Aum Shinrikyō*, Richmond (2000).

FROM SAMURAI TO SPIRIT

1   Hardacre, Helen, *Shinto and the State 1868–1988*, Princeton (1989) pp.14–15.

2   Kitagawa, Joseph M., *On Understanding Japanese Religion*, Princeton (1987) pp.165–166.

3   Hiro, Sachiya and Yamamoto, Shichibei, 'Yasukuni Shrine and the Japanese Spirit World', *Japan Echo*, 13 (1986) p.74.

4   Antoni, 'Separation of Gods', p.140.

5   Antoni, 'Separation of Gods', p.144.

6   Antoni, 'Separation of Gods', p.154.

7   Fridell, Wibur M., 'The Establishment of Shrine Shinto in Meiji Japan', *Japanese Journal of Religious Studies*, 2 (1975) p.140.

8   Hiro, 'Yasukuni', p.76.

9   Payne, Richard Karl, 'Shingon Services for the Dead' in Tanabe, George (ed.), *Religions of Japan in Practice*, Princeton (1999) pp.159–160.

10   Therefore an ordinary Japanese person who belongs to the local Sōtō Zen temple must not be assumed to spend his waking hours performing *zazen*. Instead his attitude may be more akin to the anecdote related by Ian Reader, who asked a friend which Buddhist sect he belonged to. 'I don't know,' he replied, 'no one in my family has died yet.' Reader, *Religion*, p.3.

11   Hiro, 'Yasukuni', pp.74 and 76.

12   Smith, Robert J., *Ancestor Worship in Contemporary Japan*, Stanford (1974) p.140.

13   Takashima, Shūji, 'Background on Yasukuni Shrine', *Japan Echo*, 13 (1986) pp.67–68.

14   Plath, David W., 'Where the Family of God is the Family: The Role of the Dead in Japanese Households', *American Anthropologist*, 66 (1964) p.308.

15   Payne, 'Shingon Services', p.159.

16   Smith, *Ancestor Worship*, p.41.

17   Kasahara, *A History*, p.215.

18   Hori, Ichirō, *Folk Religion in Japan: Continuity and Change*, Chicago (1968) p.123.

19   Kasahara, *A History*, p.222.

20   Thornton, Sybil, 'Epic and Religious Propaganda from the Ippen School of Pure Land Buddhism', in Tanabe, *Religions*, pp.183–192.

21   Thornton, 'Epic', p.189.

22   The Six Realms are *jigoku* (hell), *gaki* (hungry ghosts), *chikushō* (beasts), *shura* ('Titans' or 'antigods'), *ningen* (humans) and *ten* (heaven). Above these are the four heavenly states of *shōmon* (listening to the law of Buddha), *engaku* (contemplation), *bosatsu* (bodhisattva) and *butsu* (Buddhahood).

23   Lafleur, William R., 'Hungry Ghosts and Hungry People: Somaticity and Rationality in Medieval Japan', in Feher, Michel (ed.), *Fragments for a History of the Human Body, Part One*, New York (1989) pp.270–303.

24   Thornton, 'Epic', p.190.

25   Turnbull, Stephen, *Samurai Invasion: Japan's Korean War 1592–1598*, London (2002) p.206.

26   Smith, *Japan: A History in Art*, p.121.

27   Friday, Karl F., *Samurai, Warfare and the State in Early Medieval Japan*, New York (2004) p.153.

28   Friday, *Samurai, Warfare*, p.153.

29   It is precisely this belief that causes many modern Japanese to be opposed to organ removal for transplantation from someone who is brain-dead. See Morioka, Masahiro, 'Bioethics and Japanese Culture: Brain Death, Patients' Rights and Cultural Factors', *Eubios Journal of Asian and International Bioethics*, 5 (1995) pp.87–90.

30   Friday, *Samurai, Warfare*, p.153.

31   McCullough, *The Taiheiki*, p.168.

32   Takahashi, K., *Hata Sashimono*, Tokyo (1965) p.291.

33   Conlan, *State of War*, p.22.

34   Kuroda, Toshio, 'The World of Spirit Pacification: Issues of State and Religion', *Japanese Journal of Religious Studies*, 23 (1996) pp.321–351.

35   Conlan, *State of War*, p.188.

36   Colcutt, 'Religion', p.109.

37   Akamatsu, Toshihide and Yampolsky, Philip, 'Muromachi Zen and the Gozan System', in Hall, John Whitney and Toyoda, Takeshi (eds), *Japan in the Muromachi Age*, Berkeley (1977) p.314.

38   Conlan, *State of War*, p.188.

39   Rabinovitch, Judith N., *Shōmonki: The Story of Masakado's Rebellion*, Tokyo (1986).

40   Rabinovitch, *Shōmonki*, pp.138–140.

41   Rabinovitch, *Shōmonki*, pp.3–4.

42   Kuroda, 'The World', p.343.

43   Kuroda, 'The World', p.322.

44   Antoni, Klaus, 'Yasukuni Jinja and Folk Religion', in Mullins, Mark et al., *Religion and Society in Modern Japan: Selected Readings*, Berkeley (1993) p.122.

45   Sugiyama, Kyūshirō, 'Facts and Fallacies about Yasukuni Shrine', *Japan Echo*, 13 (1986) p.71.

46   Seaton, Philip, 'Reporting the 2001 Textbook and Yasukuni Shrine Controversies: Japanese War Memory and Commemoration in the British Media', *Japan Forum*, 17 (2005) p.299.

47   Gardner, Richard, 'Nationalistic Shintō: A Child's Guide to Yasukuni Shrine', in Tanabe, *Religions*, pp.334–339.

48   Hardacre, *Shinto and the State*, pp.90–91.

49   Hardacre, *Shinto and the State*, pp.91–92.

50   For a recent condemnation from the Chinese perspective see the book produced by the Modern History Institute of the Chinese Academy of Social Sciences, *Class A War Criminals Enshrined at Yasukuni Shrine*, Beijing (2005).

51   Gardner, 'Nationalistic Shintō', p.339.

52   Hiro, 'Yasukuni', p.73.

53   Kuroda, 'The World', p.323.

54   Antoni, 'Yasukuni', p.122.

55   Antoni, 'Yasukuni', p.131.

56   Sugiyama, 'Facts and Fallacies', p.69.

57   The Yūshūkan Museum devotes only one small room to pre-Meiji military history, but provides a fascinating insight into its main subject matter. The Tokkō Heiwa Kaikan (Special Attack Forces Peace Museum – i.e the Museum of the *Kamikaze*) in Chiran is also worth visiting for similar reasons.

EPILOGUE

1   Sonoda, Minoru, 'The Traditional Festival in Urban Society', *Japanese Journal of Religious Studies*, 2 (1975) pp.103–136; Nelson, John K., *A Year in the Life of a Shinto Shrine*, Washington (1996).

2   Blacker, Carmen, 'Initiation in the Shugendo: The Passage through the Ten States of Existence', in Bleeker, C. J. (ed.), *Initiation: contributions to the theme of the study-conference of the International Association for the History of Religions, held at Strasburg, September 17th to 22nd 1964*, Leiden (1965) pp.98–111; Blacker, Carmen, *The Catalpa Bow: A Study of Shamanistic Practices in Japan*, London (1975); Earhart, H. Byron, *A Religious Study of the Mount Haguro Sect of Shugendo*, Tokyo (1970); Sekimori, Gaynor, 'Shugendō: The State of the Field', *Monumenta Nipponica*, 57 (2005) pp.207–221; Swanson, Paul, 'Shugendo and the Yoshino-Kumano Pilgrimage', *Monumenta Nipponica*, 36 (1981) pp.55–84; Tyler, Royall and Swanson, Paul (eds), 'Special Edition on Shugendo', *Japanese Journal of Religious Studies*, 16, 2–13 (1989) pp.93–142.

3   Czaja, Michael, *Gods of Myth and Stone: Phallicism in Japanese Folk Religion*, New York (1974).

4   From a leaflet available at the shrine.

5   Sadler, *The Maker*, p.404.

SELECT BIBLIOGRAPHY

Adolphson, Michael, *The Gates of Power: Monks, Courtiers and Warriors in Premodern Japan*, Honolulu (2000)

Antoni, Klaus, 'The "Separation of Gods and Buddhas" at Omiwa Jinja in Meiji Japan', *Japanese Journal of Religious Studies*, 22 (1995) pp.139–159

Bitō, Masahide, 'The Akō Incident (1701–1703)', *Monumenta Nipponica*, 58 (2003) pp.149–169

Boxer, Charles, *The Christian Century in Japan 1549–1650*, Manchester (1951)

Breen, John and Teeuwen, Mark (eds), *Shinto in History: Ways of the Kami*, Richmond (2000)

Breen, John and Williams, Mark (eds), *Japan and Christianity: Impacts and Responses*, Basingstoke (1996)

Brown, Delmer M. (ed.) *The Cambridge History of Japan Volume 1, Ancient Japan*, Cambridge (1993)

Conlan, Thomas D., *State of War: The Violent Order of Fourteenth Century Japan*, Ann Arbor (2003)

Dobbins, James C., 'Editor's Introduction: Kuroda Toshio and His Scholarship', *Japanese Journal of Religious Studies*, 23 (1996) pp.218–232

Elison, George, *Deus Destroyed: The Image of Christianity in Early Modern Japan*, Harvard (1973)

Elison, George and Smith, Bardwell, L. (eds), *Warlords, Artists and Commoners: Japan in the Sixteenth Century*, Honolulu (1981)

Engel, D. H., *Japanese Gardens for Today*, Tokyo (1959)

Friday, Karl F., *Samurai, Warfare and the State in Early Medieval Japan*, New York (2004)

Grapard, Alan, 'Flying Mountains and Walkers of Emptiness: Towards a Definition of Sacred Space in Japanese Religions', *History of Religions*, 21 (1982) pp.195–221

Grayson, James H., 'Susa-no-o: A Culture Hero from Korea', *Japan Forum*, 14 (2002) pp.465–487

Hall, John Whitney and McClain, James (eds), *The Cambridge History of Japan Volume 4, Early Modern Japan*, Cambridge (1991)

Hall, John Whitney and Toyoda, Takeshi (eds), *Japan in the Muromachi Age*, Berkeley (1977)

Hardacre, Helen, *Shinto and the State 1868–1988*, Princeton (1989)

Herrigel, Eugen, *Zen in the Art of Archery*, trans. from the German by R. F. C. Hull, London (1953)

Hiro, Sachiya and Yamamoto, Shichibei, 'Yasukuni Shrine and the Japanese Spirit World', *Japan Echo*, 13 (1986) pp.73–80

Hori, Ichirō, *Folk Religion in Japan: Continuity and Change*, Chicago (1968)

Hori, Ichirō et al., *Japanese Religion: A Survey by the Agency for Cultural Affairs*, Tokyo (1972)

Hurst, G. Cameron, 'Death, Honor and Loyalty: The Bushido Ideal', *Philosophy East and West*, 40 (1990) pp.511–527

Jansen, Marius B., *Warrior Rule in Japan*, Cambridge (1995)

Kasahara, Kazuo (ed.), *A History of Japanese Religion*, Tokyo (2001)

Katō, Bunnō et al., *The Threefold Lotus Sutra*, New York (1975)

Kitagawa, Joseph, *Religion in Japanese History*, New York (1966)

Kitagawa, Joseph, *On Understanding Japanese Religion*, Princeton (1987)

Kornicki, P. F. and McMullen, I. J. (eds), *Religion in Japan: Arrows to Heaven and Earth*, Cambridge (1996)

Kuroda, Toshio, 'The World of Spirit Pacification: Issues of State and Religion', *Japanese Journal of Religious Studies*, 23 (1996) pp.321–351

McMullen, James, 'Confucian Perspectives on the Ako Revenge: Law and Moral Agency', *Monumenta Nipponica*, 58 (2003) pp.293–315

Marcure, Kenneth, 'The Danka System', *Monumenta Nipponica*, 40 (1985) pp.39–67

Marra, Michelle 'The Development of Mappo Thought in Japan (I)', *Japanese Journal of Religious Studies*, 15 (1988) pp.25–54

Mass, Jeffrey P. (ed.), *Court and Bakufu in Japan: Essays in Kamakura History*, Stanford (1982)

Mass, Jeffrey P., *The Origins of Japan's Medieval World: Courtiers, Clerics, Warriors and Peasants in the Fourteenth Century*, Stanford (1997)

Morris, Ivan, *The Nobility of Failure: Tragic Heroes in the History of Japan*, London (1975)

Mullins, Mark et al. (eds.), *Religion and Society in Modern Japan: Selected Readings*, Berkeley (1993)

Nelson, John K., 'Freedom of Expression: The Very Modern Practice of Visiting a Shinto Shrine', *Japanese Journal of Religious Studies*, 23 (1996) pp.117–153

Nelson, John K., *Enduring Identities: The Guise of Shinto in Contemporary Japan*, Honolulu (2000)

Nitobe, Inazo, *Bushido: The Soul of Japan*, New York (1905)

Nukariya, Kaiten, *The Religion of the Samurai*, London (1913)

Ooms, Herbert, *Tokugawa Ideology: Early Constructs, 1570–1680*, Princeton (1985)

Reader, Ian, *Religion in Contemporary Japan*, London (1991)

Reader, Ian, *Religious Violence in Contemporary Japan: The Case of Aum Shinrikyō*, Richmond (2000)

Reader, Ian et al., *Japanese Religions Past and Present*, Folkestone (1993)

Sadler, A. L., *Cha-no-yu the Japanese Tea Ceremony*, Rutland (1962)

Shimazu, Naoko, 'The Myth of the "Patriotic Soldier": Japanese attitudes Towards Death in the Russo-Japanese War', *War and Society* (2001) pp.69–89

Shinoda, Minoru, *The Founding of the Kamakura Shogunate 1180–1185, with selective translations from the Azuma Kagami*, New York (1960)

Shively, Donald H. and McCullough, William (eds), *The Cambridge History of Japan Volume 2, Heian Japan*, Cambridge (1999)

Stone, Jacqueline, 'Rebuking the Enemies of the *Lotus*: Nichirenist Exclusivism in Historical Perspective', *Japanese Journal of Religious Studies*, 21 (1994) pp.231–259

Suzuki, D. T., *Zen and Japanese Culture*, Princeton (1970)

Tanabe, George (ed.), *Religions of Japan in Practice*, Princeton (1999)

Teeuwen, Mark and Scheid, Bernhard, 'Tracing Shinto in the History of Kami Worship', *Japanese Journal of Religious Studies*, 29 (2000) pp.195–207

Tsunoda, Ryusaku et al. *Sources of Japanese Tradition*, Vols 1 and 2, New York (1964)

Tucker, John Allen, 'Rethinking the Ako Ronin Debate: The Religious Significance of Chūshin gishi', *Japanese Journal of Religious Studies*, 26 (1999) pp.1–37

Turnbull, Stephen, *The Kakure Kirishitan of Japan: A Study of their Development, Beliefs and Rituals to the Present Day*, Folkestone (1998)

Tyler, Royall, 'Buddhism in Noh', *Japanese Journal of Religious Studies*, 14 (1987) pp.19–52

Tyler, Royall and Swanson, Paul (eds), 'Special Edition on Shugendo', *Japanese Journal of Religious Studies*, 16, 2–13 (1989) pp.93–142

Tyler, Susan, 'Honji Suijaku Faith', *Japanese Journal of Religious Studies*, 16 (1989) pp.227–250

Von Durkheim, Karlfried, *The Japanese Cult of Tranquillity*, London (1974)

Yamada, Shoji, 'The Myth of Zen in the Art of Archery', *Japanese Journal of Religious Studies*, 28 (2001) pp.1–30

Yamamoto, Tsunetomo, *The Book of the Samurai: Hagakure*, trans. by William Scott Wilson, Tokyo (1979)

GLOSSARY

Amaterasu	the Shintō 'Sun-Goddess'
ankokuji	temples for the war dead
bosatsu	a bodhisattva; one who is dedicated to assisting all sentient beings achieve complete Buddhahood
bushidō	the way of the warrior
butsudan	family Buddhist altar
chadō	the way of tea
chū	loyalty
daimyō	warlord
Dainichi	the 'great' or 'central' Buddha
danka	temple registration system under the Tokugawa
dogū	clay figures of females dating from the Jōmon Period
dōtaku	bronze bell-shaped artefacts dating from the Yayoi Period
eboshi	a cap worn by courtiers and samurai
feng shui	Chinese geomancy
Four Noble Truths	the fundamental insight or enlightenment of Buddha, relating to the existence of suffering and its cessation
fumi-e	image trampling to reveal secret Christians
goryō shinkō	vengeful spirits
goshintai	the object that houses a *kami* in a shrine
gunkimono	war tales
Hachiman	the Shintō god of war
hondō	the main hall of a Buddhist temple
hongan	original vow of Amida Buddha
honji suijaku	theory that Buddha manifested himself as the *kami*
ihai	memorial tablet
jingū-ji	shrine/temple complex
jinja	a Shintō shrine
junshi	following in death by suicide
kaihyōgō	'marathon' pilgrimage on Mount Hiei
Kakure Kirishitan	Hidden Christians
kami	gods of Shintō
kami kaze	divine wind
kamidana	god shelf in the home
kannushi	a Shintō priest
kare-sansui	dry landscape garden
kata	style or form

kengō	master swordsman
Kirishitan	Christian of the 16th century
kō	filial piety
kōan	theme or problem in Zen
kofun	large burial mounds
kokugaku	national learning
kyūdō	Japanese archery
mandala	artistic presentation of Buddhism
mappō	age of descent into chaos
matsuri	Shintō shrine festival
mikkyō	esoteric Buddhism
mikoshi	portable shrine
monto	disciple or believer
mujō	impermanence of all phenomena
musha shūgyō	warrior pilgrimage
nembutsu	invoking Amida's name in prayer
norito	Shintō prayers
onryō	angry ghost
rōnin	masterless samurai
sabi	appreciation of that which is old, faded and rustic
senpuku Kirishitan	secret Christians under the Tokugawa
seppuku	suicide by disembowelment (*hara kiri*)
shaku	the wooden wand carried by Shintō priests
shikken	regency
shimenawa	the rope used to enclose sacred spaces in Shintō
shintai	same as *goshintai*
Shintō	religious system concerned with the worship of *kami*
Shogun	the military dictator of Japan from 1192 to 1868
shōji	sliding paper screens
sōhei	warrior monk or priest soldier
sutra	Buddhist scriptures
Taoism	a belief system formulated in China by Laozi in the 5th century BC
torii	shrine gateway in the shape of the Greek letter 'pi'
ujiko	shrine adherents
wabi	quietness and tranquillity
yamabushi	mountain ascetic
yamato damashii	spirit of Japan
yūgen	mystery
zazen	sitting in meditation

INDEX

References to illustrations are shown in **bold**.